27-9

Reiner Wehle

Clarinet Fundamentals
Basisübungen für Klarinette

Volume 1: Sound and Articulation
Band 1: Klangübungen und Artikulation

ED 9882
ISMN: 979-0-001-13934-2

www.schott-music.com

Mainz · London · Berlin · Madrid · New York · Paris · Prague · Tokyo · Toronto
© 2007 SCHOTT MUSIC GmbH & Co. KG, Mainz · Printed in Germany

Contents

Inhalt

Impressum:

Bestellnummer: ED 9882
ISMN: 979-0-001-13934-2
ISBN: 978-3-7957-5804-2
Englische Übersetzung: Victoria Viebahn
Fotos: Reiner Wehle
Lektorat: Dr. Rainer Mohrs
© 2007 Schott Music GmbH & Co. KG, Mainz
Printed in Germany · BSS 51 835

Preface

When listening to music, we are very often fascinated and inspired by the virtuosity and sometimes near-superhuman technical mastery displayed on a musical instrument. However justified and natural this admiration for exceptional virtuosity may be, any discerning person will be equally aware that it cannot represent music's sole purpose. After all, many of the finest and most moving works given to us by the great composers are not, technically and manually speaking, among the especially demanding ones to play. But in the interpretation of one particular artist a slow movement by Mozart, for example, will mysteriously radiate life, transporting the composer's spirit and emotions into the present, whereas in the hands of others this is clearly not the case. The difference obviously lies not in the number and tempo of the notes played, but in the tonal sensitivity and the greatest possible ability to differentiate, two playing characteristics that are mutually interdependent. This is a matter of active creation and conscious connection of tones, and the quality of the sounds, as opposed to (merely) their quantity. The possibilities offered by just a single note in terms of its beginning, its tone colours, its dynamic nuances and its termination are endless! The development of such possibilities should not, and indeed must not, be left to chance. Training that claims to do justice to artistic standards must see to it that they are cultivated and perfected wisely and thoroughly. For the clarinettist, this means that the processes involved in breathing, breathing support, and breath control in the mouth cavity, the forming of syllables to colour the tone, the choice of embouchure position and pressure on the reed, and the mobility of the tongue all require training just as intensive as that needed to achieve free-flowing processes in finger technique and clean, responsive intonation.

Years of teaching have shown me that many of these areas are given only meagre consideration in the well-known clarinet instruction manuals. These "Clarinet Fundamentals" came into being – hand in hand with my practical work as a teacher – to close the gaps.

All three volumes are directed at young advanced pupils and music students, but it also makes extremely good sense to integrate many of the exercises into lessons for beginners. In the areas of legato, intonation, finger-work training and, above all, sound exercises, it is of the utmost importance to begin with the easiest processes and build up the practice programme systematically. Using the "Clarinet Fundamentals", it is possible to develop a natural and easy relationship with the instrument from the very start. Nothing stands more in the way of successful learning than exaggerated demands, negative experiences, and fear!

The "Clarinet Fundamentals" are, on the one hand, suited for use as a progressive learning programme. On the other hand, many of the exercises, in particular the sound exercises and the fingering course also offer the player the chance to keep up the standard reached on a lasting (and effective) basis. For this reason, the "Clarinet Fundamentals" can also be of value to professionals, especially in view of the fact that in some areas (such as fingering on the bass clarinet/basset horn/basset clarinet, or intonation), exercises of this type are scarcely to

Vorwort

Immer wieder ist man als Musikhörer fasziniert und begeistert über die virtuose, manchmal nahezu menschenunmögliche Beherrschung eines Musikinstruments. So legitim und natürlich es ist, diese äußerste Virtuosität aufrichtig zu bewundern, so klar dürfte jedem verständigen Menschen jedoch auch sein, dass in ihr nicht der alleinige Sinn von Musik liegen kann, gehören doch gerade viele manuell-technisch nicht anspruchsvolle Werke zum Schönsten und Ergreifendsten, welches uns die großen Komponisten hinterlassen haben. Wenn also beispielsweise ein langsamer Satz von Mozart bei einem bestimmten Interpreten auf rätselhafte Weise Leben ausstrahlt und Geist und Emotionen des Komponisten in die Gegenwart übermittelt und bei anderen Spielern so ganz offensichtlich nicht, dann liegt der Unterschied sicher nicht in Anzahl und Tempo der gespielten Noten, sondern vor allem in der Sensibilisierung für den Klang und in der Fähigkeit zu höchstmöglicher Differenzierung, Eigenschaften, die sich beide gegenseitig bedingen. Es geht darum, Töne aktiv zu formen und bewußt zu verbinden, es geht um die Qualität der Klänge und nicht (nur) um die Quantität. Welche unendlichen Möglichkeiten bietet schon der einzelne Ton mit seinem Einschwingen, seinen Klangfarben, seinen dynamischen Schattierungen und seinem Verklingen! Diese Möglichkeiten sollen und dürfen sich aber nicht durch Zufall entwickeln, sondern müssen in einer Ausbildung, welche künstlerischen Maßstäben gerecht werden soll, klug und gründlich gefördert und entwickelt werden. Für den Klarinettisten bedeutet dies, dass alle Vorgänge der Atmung, der Atemstütze, der Luftführung im Mundraum, der Vokalformung bei der Tonfärbung, die Wahl des Ansatzpunktes und des Ansatzdruckes am Klarinettenblatt sowie die geschickte Beweglichkeit der Zunge genauso intensiver Ausbildung bedürfen wie alle lockeren Bewegungsabläufe der Fingertechnik und eine bewußte, saubere Intonation.

Meine langjährige pädagogische Tätigkeit hat mir gezeigt, dass viele dieser Bereiche in den bekannten Schulwerken für Klarinette nur unzureichend behandelt werden. Um diese Lücke zu schließen, entstanden in enger Verbindung mit der praktischen pädagogischen Tätigkeit die vorliegenden "Basisübungen für Klarinette".

Alle drei Bände wenden sich an fortgeschrittene Schüler einer Musikschule und an Musikstudenten. Viele der Übungen können aber auch sehr sinnvoll in den Anfängerunterricht integriert werden. In den Bereichen Legato, Intonation, Griffschule und vor allem bei den Klangübungen ist es ungemein wichtig, mit den einfachsten Vorgängen zu beginnen und das Übungsprogramm systematisch aufzubauen. Mit den "Basisübungen für Klarinette" ist es möglich, von Beginn an ein unverkrampftes, natürliches Verhältnis zum Instrument zu entwickeln. Nichts ist schädlicher für den Lernerfolg als Überforderung, negative Erfahrung und Angst!

Die "Basisübungen für Klarinette" eignen sich einerseits als fortschreitender Ausbildungsgang, andererseits bieten viele der Übungen, gerade bei den Klangübungen und in der Griffschule die Möglichkeit, sich ein erarbeitetes Niveau dauerhaft (und effektiv) zu erhalten. Daher können die "Basisübungen für Klarinette" auch für professionelle Bläser von Nutzen sein,

be found elsewhere. Nevertheless, the volumes are not intended to replace the good teaching works but simply to complement them. They should not on any account be regarded as dogma; rather, they may be woven into the clarinettist's training in a flexible and individual fashion. Thus used, I am convinced that for many clarinettists – teachers and pupils alike – the "Clarinet Fundamentals" will open up paths to effective practice.

The "Clarinet Fundamentals" were written in close artistic and pedagogic collaboration with my wife, the world-famous clarinettist Sabine Meyer, to whom I am indebted and grateful for countless valuable ideas, artistic impulses and constructive discussions. I would also like to thank Jens Thoben (Principal Clarinettist at the Deutsche Oper am Rhein), who, as a former student at the Lübeck Music College, experienced most of the exercises 'in the flesh' and to whom I am grateful for a large number of suggestions for improvement and help with wording. I am well aware that attempting to put many of the tonal and artistic intentions of these exercises into theoretical terms is problematic. From the language perspective, the aim has been to describe all processes with as much precision as possible, so that the careful reader will be rewarded with some valuable and thought-provoking insights and, through listening, will be able to understand the sense of what he or she has read.

When learning an instrument, the better one can listen to one's own playing, the better the results!

Finally, I would like to thank Victoria Viebahn for all the work involved in providing an informed translation.

Reiner Wehle

zumal einige Bereiche (wie Griffübungen für Bassklarinette/Bassetthorn/Bassettklarinette oder Intonationsübungen) in dieser Art kaum anderswo verfügbar sind. Trozdem sollen die vorliegende Bände die guten Schulwerke für Klarinette nicht ersetzen sondern nur ergänzen. Sie sollen auch auf keinen Fall ein Dogma darstellen, sondern bieten die Möglichkeit, flexibel und individuell in den Ausbildungsgang integriert zu werden. Ich bin sicher, dass die „Basisübungen für Klarinette", auf diese Weise genutzt, vielen Klarinettisten – Lehrern wie Schülern – Wege zu effektivem Üben eröffnen werden.

Die „Basisübungen für Klarinette" entstanden in enger künstlerischen und pädagogischer Zusammenarbeit mit meiner Frau – der weltbekannten Klarinettistin Sabine Meyer –, der ich für unzählige, wertvolle Anregungen, künstlerische Ansprüche und konstruktive Gespräche großen Dank schulde. Desweiteren verdanke ich Herrn Jens Thoben (Soloklarinettist der Deutschen Oper am Rhein), der als ehemaliger Student der Musikhochschule Lübeck die meisten Übungen praktisch miterlebt hat, eine große Zahl von Verbesserungsvorschlägen und Formulierungshilfen. Mir ist bewußt, dass ein großer Teil der klanglichen und künstlerischen Intentionen dieser Übungen nur schwer theoretisch zu fixieren sind. Es wurde versucht, alle Vorgänge sprachlich möglichst exakt zu erfassen, so dass der aufmerksame Leser den einen oder anderen wertvollen Denkanstoß erhalten und durch die Hörerfahrung den Sinn nachempfinden kann.

Das Erlernen eines Instruments gelingt umso besser, je besser man es versteht, sich selber zuzuhören!

Eine letzter Dank gebührt Frau Victoria Viebahn für die große Arbeit der fachkundigen Übersetzung.

Reiner Wehle

Almost anyone who learns to play a musical instrument will agree: Playing the instrument is enjoyable and so – normally – are the lessons with the teacher. But as for the "practising"! How often has one had to force oneself to practise, how often has one failed to find the motivation to do so and how many minutes of practice have seemed tortuously endless? Is practising simply a most vexing business?

On the other hand, every instrumental teacher is familiar with the case of pupils not always making the progress that could be expected of them. There are the highly talented pupils who practise for hours on end but seem merely to go round in circles, and others with moderate talent who make surprisingly rapid headway. The only obvious general message in such situations is that the reason must lie in the way they practise. But how can "practising" be practised?

These days, good books are available on this subject, but a teaching album of "Clarinet Fundamentals" must at least set out some basic principles so that anyone opting to make use of it has the opportunity to reflect on his or her own approach to practising:

(1) To make sense, any practice requires an aim

The following questions should be asked before each practice session:
- What do I want to improve today (or this week)? Which improvements can I achieve today (or this week)? The tasks one sets oneself might not be large enough, but equally, they might be too large.
- Which exercise is appropriate for achieving the aim? Which interim steps will bring me closer to my goal? What exactly are the intended aims of the exercise my teacher has given me to work on?
- Am I already playing the way I mean to play? Whereabouts in the exercise am I not yet playing as I would like to?
- **Am I actually practising elements I intend to improve on or simply playing through what I can play already?**
- A positive attitude is an integral part of good practice, so it is important that one is aware of the progress that one has made and is pleased with it!

(2) Good practice requires concentration

Concentration can be practised too. The important points are:
- Avoid practising when overtired. Avoid practising in stuffy, poorly-ventilated rooms. Avoid practising immediately after eating a main meal.
- **Practise in an environment where there is peace and quiet!** No noise from outside, no television, no radio and no mobile phone!
- If one is thinking of other things while practising, one is not practising properly. Practising without thinking leads to automatic processes that can be very harmful.

Fast jeder, der das Spielen eines Musikinstruments erlernt, wird zustimmen, dass das Spielen des Instruments Freude bereitet und der Unterricht bei einem Lehrer meist auch. Aber das „Üben"! Wie oft hat man sich zum Üben zwingen müssen, wie oft hat man sich nicht aufraffen können und wie viele Minuten hat man beim Üben als quälend lang empfunden! Ist das Üben also ein großes Ärgernis?

Auf der anderen Seite hat sicher jeder Instrumentallehrer schon die Erfahrung gemacht, dass Schüler nicht immer den Fortschritt machen, den man von ihnen erwarten würde. Es gibt hochtalentierte Schüler, die viele Stunden üben und trotzdem irgendwie auf der Stelle treten und es gibt mittlere Begabungen, die überraschend schnell vorankommen. Klar ist in solchen Momenten meist nur, dass es an der Art des Übens liegen muss. Doch wie kann man das „Üben" üben?

Es gibt mittlerweile gute Bücher über dieses Thema, doch ist es sicher notwendig, in einem Schulwerk mit „Basisübungen für Klarinette" zumindest einige Grundregeln des Übens aufzuzeigen, damit jedem, der dieses Heft nutzen möchte, die Gelegenheit gegeben wird, sich über das eigene Üben Gedanken zu machen:

(1) Jedes sinnvolle Üben braucht ein Ziel

Folgende Fragen sollten vor jedem Üben gestellt werden:
- Was will ich heute (und in dieser Woche) verbessern? Wie viel kann ich heute (und in dieser Woche) an Verbesserungen erreichen? Man kann sich zu kleine Aufgaben stellen, aber auch zu große.
- Welche Übung ist geeignet, das Ziel zu erreichen? Welche Zwischenschritte bringen mich dem Ziel näher? Was will die Übung, die der Lehrer aufgab, konkret verbessern?
- Spiele ich schon so, wie ich es mir vorstelle? An welcher Stelle der Übung spiele ich noch nicht so, wie ich möchte?
- **Übe ich die Dinge, die ich verbessern will, oder spiele ich nur, was ich sowieso schon kann?**
- Zum guten Üben gehört eine positive Einstellung. Es ist daher auch wichtig, sich nach dem Üben die erreichten Verbesserungen klar zu machen und sich darüber zu freuen!

(2) Gutes Üben braucht Konzentration

Auch Konzentration kann geübt werden. Wichtig ist:
- Nicht üben, wenn man übermüdet ist. Nicht in schlecht belüfteten Räumen üben. Nicht direkt nach den Hauptmahlzeiten üben.
- **Üben, wo man Ruhe hat!** Kein Lärm von draußen, kein Fernseher, kein Radio und auch kein Handy.
- Wer beim Üben an andere Dinge denkt, übt falsch. Gedankenloses Üben führt zu Automatismen, die sehr schädlich sein können.

— Difficult processes, in particular, can only be learned effectively if the fine points can be monitored carefully. Consequently, one should ask the following questions: "What exactly happens just before the mistake takes place? What exactly must I do just before the critical point to avoid making the mistake?" Only following intelligent analysis can one master complex passages and learn not to fear them.

— It is most helpful to practise a difficult passage mentally, without music or instrument to hand. Each movement of the body is steered consciously or unconsciously by the brain. If one is able to imagine the notes, tone colours and movement sequences without the instrument, their actual realisation is no longer difficult. But mental practice also takes some learning!

3 Mechanical practice is to be avoided

— The practice programme must be flexible and full of variety, so that one can keep up one's attention throughout. Practising should be neither monotonous and stereotyped nor lacking in a precise plan. Resolutions such as: "Now I'm going to play that through twelve times" are generally a pointless waste of time – time which could be better spent.

— Some passages improve substantially when during the course of the practice the articulation or the rhythm is varied or accents added.

— "Interval training" is useful, both in the order of the items to be practised and also in the choice of tempo.

— In longer passages being practised, the important thing is to pinpoint exactly where the difficulties, and thus the errors, might lie.

— **Above all, one has to recognize the point when an exercise is no longer bringing any progress, at least for the time being!**

4 Never practise unmusically!

— All music is structured in phrases. In music, uniform sequences of sounds exist only as exceptions. Even scales and finger exercises are organised meaningfully, according to their metre. All sequences of action must therefore be organic. Organic sequences also require that the whole body, without stiffness, is involved in the playing.

— **Each and every note, with its beginning, sounding and ending, already constitutes music!**

— In technical exercises, the results achieved are considerably better if the player is careful to produce a cultivated and controlled tone.

— Gerade schwierige Abläufe lernt man nur effektiv, wenn man die Details aufmerksam beobachten kann. Folgende Fragen sollte man sich daher stellen: „Was genau geschieht, bevor der Fehler auftritt? Was genau muss ich vor dem Fehler tun, um den Fehler zu vermeiden?" Erst durch kluge Analyse lernt man, die komplizierte Passagen zu beherrschen und nicht, sie zu fürchten.

— Es ist sehr hilfreich, gerade schwierige Stellen mental zu üben, ohne die Noten, ohne das Instrument. Jede Körperbewegung wird bewusst oder unbewusst vom Gehirn gesteuert. Wenn man sich daher Töne, Klangfarben und Bewegungsabläufe ohne das Instrument geistig vorstellen kann, ist die Praxis ncht mehr schwierig. Aber auch mentales Üben will gelernt sein!

3 Man vermeide, mechanisch zu üben

— Das Übeprogramm sollte abwechslungsreich und flexibel sein, damit man immer aufmerksam sein kann. Man sollte also weder monoton und stereotyp üben, noch ohne eine genaue Planung. Vorsätze wie: „Ich spiele das jetzt zwölfmal durch", sind meist sinnlos vergeudete Zeit, die man besser nutzen könnte.

— Manche Stellen verbessern sich ganz wesentlich durch Änderung der Artikulation beim Übungsablauf, durch Rhythmisierungen oder durch Hinzufügen von Akzenten.

— Ein „Intervalltraining" sowohl in der Abfolge der Übungsteile, als auch in der Tempowahl ist hilfreich.

— Wichtig ist, in größeren Übungsteilen zu erkennen, wo genau die Schwierigkeiten liegen und daher Fehler auftreten könnten.

— **Man muss vor allem merken, wann eine Übung im Moment keine Fortschritte mehr bringt!**

4 Man übe nie unmusikalisch

— Jede Musik ist in Phrasen strukturiert. Gleichförmige Klangereignisse gibt es in der Musik nur als Ausnahme. Auch Tonleitern oder Fingerübungen sind durch ein Metrum sinnvoll gegliedert. Alle Abläufe müssen daher organisch sein. Organische Abläufe bedeuten auch, den ganzen Körper beim Spiel unverkrampft mit einzubeziehen.

— **Jeder einzelne Ton ist mit seinem Beginn, seinem Klang und seinem Ende schon Musik!**

— Technische Übungen gelingen wesentlich besser, wenn man auf einen gepflegten, kontrollierten Ton achtet.

5 Attention must be given to good posture (see also under "Breathing and Posture")

– As the instrument is played using not only the fingers but the entire body, the player's standing (or indeed sitting) position should be straight and not hollow-backed, with an inner tension – but still loosely supple. Anyone who is too tired to stand properly should stop practising.
– The head faces forward rather than downward, allowing the throat area to remain open.
– The shoulders, arms, wrists and hands should be as loose as possible. The intensity of breathing should not result in the shoulders, arms and hands becoming tensed up. **The intensity of wind playing and the looseness of the arms are not naturally contradictory!**
– Holding the instrument often impinges on the looseness of the right hand, in particular. It can be helpful in this case to use a sling – at least temporarily – or to practise sitting down with the clarinet supported slightly.

6 Avoid the typical practice mistakes

– If time is short, it is better to practise a small number of exercises properly than to half-practise numerous ones!
– Regular practice is considerably more effective than practising less often but for a longer period. (It is better to practise for half an hour every day than for two hours every four days).
– Do not leave starting to practise until it is too late. Beginning a day before the lesson, three days before the exam or a week before the competition is far too late and creates great psychological pressure which could be avoided.
– One must be able to identify the most difficult passages in advance and also know how fast one will be able to play them. The tempo of any exercise is determined by the most difficult passages it contains.
– Always practise precisely in the planned rhythm.
– Always practise slowly enough to maintain freedom from tenseness. This freedom from tenseness is the tempo guide!
– Only practise each exercise as long as is necessary. Experience shows that it is not possible to concentrate on a problem for much more than 10 minutes at a time.
– **Avoid making the same mistake several times over!** Very often it is the problem that is being practised, rather than the solution!
– If a difficult passage is not turning out perfectly, instead of going from the top time and again, practise that difficult passage plus a short transitional passage leading up to it.
– Be careful to avoid the trap of practising a passage well and then playing it through one last time faster – but then imprecisely. It would be better to do the reverse.
– If one finds oneself in a crisis situation when nothing is working out well any more, it is best to stop practising and go for a walk instead!

5 Man achte auf eine allgemein gute Körperhaltung (siehe auch bei „Atmung und Haltung")

– Da man sein Instrument nicht nur mit den Fingern, sondern mit dem ganzen Körper spielt, sollte man gespannt – aber trotzdem locker –, aufrecht, gerade und ohne Hohlkreuz stehen (oder auch sitzen). Wer zu müde ist, um noch gut zu stehen, der sollte nicht mehr üben.
– Der Kopf schaut nach vorn und nicht nach unten, damit der Halsbereich offen bleibt.
– Schultern, Arme, Handgelenke und Hände sollen so locker wie möglich sein. Die Intensität der Atemführung darf nicht zu festen Schultern, Armen und Händen führen. **Bläserische Spannung und Lockerheit der Arme sind kein naturgegebener Gegensatz!**
– Das Halten des Instruments behindert häufig die Lockerheit gerade der rechten Hand. Es kann dann günstig sein – wenigstens vorübergehend –, einen Tragegurt zu benutzen oder auch im Sitzen zu üben und die Klarinette etwas abzustützen.

6 Man vermeide die typischen Übefehler

– Wenn man wenig Zeit hat, ist es besser, wenige Übungen gut zu üben, als viele Übungen nur halb!
– Regelmäßiges Üben ist wesentlich effektiver als seltenes, dann aber längeres Üben. (Es ist besser, jeden Tag eine halbe Stunde zu üben, als alle vier Tage zwei Stunden).
– Man beginne nicht zu spät mit dem Üben. Einen Tag vor dem Unterricht, drei Tage vor der Prüfung oder eine Woche vor dem Wettbewerb sind viel zu spät und bilden einen großen, aber vermeidbaren psychischen Druck.
– Man muss die schwierigsten Stellen vorher erkennen können, und auch wissen, wie schnell man sie wird spielen können. Das Tempo jeder Übung richtet sich nach den schwersten Stellen.
– Man übe immer im genauen, geplanten Rhythmus.
– Man übe immer langsam genug, um locker bleiben zu können. Das Tempo folgt der Lockerheit!
– Man übe jede Übung nur so lange wie nötig. Erfahrungsgemäß kann man sich nicht viel länger als 10 Minuten auf ein Problem konzentrieren.
– **Man vermeide, die gleichen Fehler mehrmals zu machen!** Sehr häufig wird das Problem eingeübt und nicht die Lösung!
– Man beginne, wenn eine schwierige Stelle nicht gelingt, nicht immer wieder am Anfang des Stückes, sondern übe die schwierige Stelle und einen kurzen Übergang vor der Stelle.
– Man hüte sich davor, eine gut geübte Passage zuletzt noch einmal schneller und dann ungenau durchzuspielen. Das Gegenteil wäre besser.
– Wenn man eine Krise hat und nichts mehr gelingen will, hört man am besten auf zu üben und geht spazieren!

⑦ **Devise an intelligent individual practice programme**

There are many diverse areas of clarinet training, each of which has to be focused on separately:
– Controlling the sound (attack, steady breath control, tone colour, dynamic gradation)
– Playing a well-prepared legato with awareness
– Articulation (light staccato with good tone, portato, accents, etc)
– Intonation
– Clarinet fingering with its many tricky particularities
– Scales, arpeggios and intervals
– Studies involving the modulations of the classical/romantic harmonic system
– Studies with an extended harmonic range
– Contemporary music with special playing techniques
– Transposition
– Sight-reading
– Orchestral studies
– Daily exercises for keeping up technique
– And, of course, the end to be served by all these means: The infinitely rich clarinet repertoire!

The purpose of these volumes of "Clarinet Fundamentals" is to provide systematic practice programmes for the areas of legato, tone cultivation, articulation, intonation and the development and maintenance of supple finger technique, with the aim of raising the effectiveness of practice. **These albums are not intended to result in *"especially large amounts"* of practice but in practice that is *"especially good"*!** Good practice brings about noticeable progress which in turn generates satisfaction, security and confidence! Anyone practising systematically and creatively will soon see for themselves:
Good practice is enjoyable!

⑦ **Man entwickle ein eigenes, kluges Übeprogramm**

Es gibt verschiedene Bereiche der klarinettistischen Ausbildung, die alle einzeln trainiert werden müssen:
– die kontrollierte Beherrschung des Klangs (Anblasen, stabile Atemkontrolle, Klangfarben, dynamische Abstufungen)
– das bewusst geführte, differenzierte Legato
– die Artikulation (ein lockeres, klangschönes Staccato, Portato, Akzente etc.)
– die Intonation
– die klarinettistische Grifftechnik mit den vielen schwierigen Besonderheiten
– Tonleitern, Akkorde und Intervalle
– Etüden mit den Modulationen im klassisch-romantischen Harmoniesystem
– Etüden mit erweiterter Harmonik
– zeitgenössische Musik mit speziellen Spieltechniken
– das Transponieren
– das Vom-Blatt-Spiel
– Orchesterstudien
– tägliche Übungen zum Erhalt der Technik
– und natürlich der Zweck, dem die angegebenen Mittel dienen sollen: Die unendlich reichhaltige Klarinetten-Literatur!

Die vorliegenden Bände mit „Basisübungen für Klarinette" möchten für die Bereiche Legato, Klangschulung, Artikulation, Intonation und Aufbau und Erhalt einer lockeren Fingertechnik systematische Übungsprogramme bieten, welche die Effektivität des Übens steigern sollen. **Ziel der Bände ist es nicht, „besonders viel" zu üben, sondern „besonders gut"!** Denn gutes Üben bringt erkennbare Fortschritte und dies wiederum schafft Befriedigung, Sicherheit und Selbstvertrauen! Wer mit Systematik und Kreativität übt, wird bald erkennen: **Gutes Üben macht Freude!**

Breathing and posture together make up an inseparable unit. Without good posture it is impossible to breathe well. Breathing and posture therefore also provide the starting point and basis for mastering the instrument in terms of technique and sound. The clarinet is not played using the fingers or embouchure alone, but using the entire body. True mastery of the instrument begins only when all the relevant technical processes such as finger technique and embouchure retreat well into the background behind all the holistic and natural body movements and processes involved in breathing. Then, and only then, is the player no longer 'being mastered' by the instrument!

Experience shows that this level of perfection is attainable only for the few. The possible sources of error seem infinite. A good teacher will certainly be needed, even though there is extensive literature available on tackling deep-seated problems on the subject of breathing and posture, and there are some excellent specialists at work in this field. But the most serious mistakes and postural problems must be noted here in "Clarinet Fundamentals" nonetheless. This is because first of all, without organic body behaviour it will not be possible to obtain an optimal sound, and secondly, the whole point of tone, legato and articulation exercises is to get rid of false posture and tensions, through concentrated observation and sensitivity towards the body, conscious control of breathing depth and rhythm and constant critical monitoring of the sound, employing both the ear and the mind.

In principle, where posture and breathing are concerned it makes little sense to go into too much detail examining individual parts of the body. A better approach would be to prevent or solve the problems by working towards a wholly natural posture embodying tension but not stiffness. Nevertheless, the most serious and, alas, all-too-common errors will be described below.

1 Breathing errors

Breathing is a holistic process greatly affected by mental influences. Preconditions for good, deep breathing are, therefore, a favourable psychological state and an upright posture with inner tension but flexibility. The breathing is then controlled and carried out to a significant extent by the diaphragm, in combination with the trunk muscles. In the case of so-called "full breathing", in addition to the abdominal cavity, the chest, which can be extended by means of the intercostal muscles, is also involved. But a very common mistake is to breathe primarily in the chest. This is usually associated with fear on the part of the player, whose shoulders are often hunched up. In this situation, a good pedagogue will ensure that there is a pleasant lesson atmosphere, carry out some relaxation exercises, avoid giving the pupil tasks that are too hard and make repeated postural corrections by having the pupil let his arms hang loosely at his side. When the instru-

Atmung und Haltung bilden eine untrennbare Einheit. Ohne eine gute Haltung ist es unmöglich, gut zu atmen. Atmung und Körperhaltung sind daher auch Ausgangspunkt und Basis für die technische und klangliche Beherrschung des Instruments. Klarinette spielt man nicht nur mit den Fingern oder dem Ansatz, sondern mit dem ganzen Körper. Die wirkliche Beherrschung eines Instruments beginnt erst dann, wenn alle relevanten technischen Abläufe wie Fingertechnik und Ansatz gegenüber allen ganzheitlichen, natürlichen Körperbewegungen und Atemabläufen deutlich in den Hintergrund geraten. Erst dann wird man nicht mehr von seinem Instrument beherrscht!

Die Erfahrung zeigt, dass diese Stufe der Vollkommenheit nur wenigen erreichbar ist. Die Quelle für Fehler scheint unendlich. Man wird sicher nicht ohne die Hilfe eines guten Pädagogen auskommen, wobei es zum Thema Haltung und Atmung bei tiefsitzenden Problemen auch umfangreiche Fachliteratur und ausgezeichnete Spezialisten gibt. Trotzdem müssen in diesen „Basisübungen für Klarinette" die wichtigsten Fehler und Fehlhaltungen angesprochen werden, denn erstens wird sich ohne organisches Körperverhalten nicht der optimale Klang einstellen und zweitens liegt der Sinn von Klang-, Legato- und Artikulationsübungen gerade darin, dass man über konzentriertes Beobachten und Erfühlen seines Körpers, über bewusstes Steuern von Atemtiefe und Atemrhythmus und über die ständige kritische Kontrolle des Klangs durch Ohr und Bewusstsein eine Reinigung von Fehlhaltungen und Anspannungen erreicht.

Im Prinzip ist es nicht sinnvoll, wenn man sich in Bezug auf Haltung und Atmung zu sehr in Details und einzelne Körperregionen vertieft. Es wäre besser, die Probleme zu verhindern oder zu lösen, indem man auf eine insgesamt natürliche, gespannte aber nicht verkrampfte Körperhaltung hinarbeiten würde. Trotzdem sollen hier die schwerwiegendsten und leider weit verbreiteten Fehler aufgezeigt werden.

1 Atemfehler

Die Atmung ist ein ganzheitlicher Vorgang, der großen psychischen Einflüssen ausgesetzt ist. Eine gute und tiefe Atmung setzt daher eine gute psychische Verfassung und eine gespannte, aufgerichtete, aber lockere Haltung voraus. Die Atmung wird dann zu wesentlichen Teilen vom Zwerchfell in Verbindung mit der Rumpfmuskulatur gesteuert und ausgeführt. Bei der sogenannten „Vollatmung" ist neben dem Bauchraum auch der Brustraum beteiligt, der sich mit Hilfe der Zwischenrippenmuskeln weiten kann. Ein sehr häufiger Fehler ist aber, dass überwiegend im Brustraum geatmet wird. Dies hängt wesentlich damit zusammen, dass der Spieler Angst hat und die Schultern hochzieht. Ein guter Pädagoge wird in diesem Fall für eine angenehme Unterrichtsatmosphäre sorgen, Lockerungsübungen einbeziehen, dem Schüler nicht zu schwierige Aufgaben stellen und immer wie-

ment is brought up to play once more, the shoulder area should not, indeed must not, be allowed to rise again.

A further breathing error comes from the fact that far too little attention is given to **breathing out** well during the rests. In most cases, when playing the clarinet one has not too little air but generally too much, and one fails to take the time to breathe out the air not needed for playing. (Soft reeds, in particular, can be extremely exhausting in this context!) Compared to normal breathing, therefore, it is the breathing rhythm that is quite different. For the pupil to learn to breathe out the leftover air as far as possible before taking a breath, suppleness and relaxation are required. These should be the target of every wind player's training from the very start.

Closely associated with the breathing is the **breathing support.** The wind player's breathing support fulfils three main functions: Firstly, it stabilises the body posture by means of the abdominal muscles, especially when the body loses tension when releasing a large amount of air; secondly, it ensures control and evenness of air release, which is of elemental importance in the case of very long, very soft or very high notes; and thirdly, in a finely-tuned interplay of diaphragm, trunk muscles and intercostal muscles on the one hand and embouchure tension and opening of the larynx on the other, it ensures that the air pressure is optimal for playing the instrument. But it is precisely here that lack of knowledge still leads to the majority of mistakes being made. Pressing strongly in the abdominal cavity (whether inwards or outwards), extending the abdomen (see under "Hollow back") and general hardening of the abdominal wall have nothing whatsoever to do with "good support", result in far too much pressure and above all have the fatal effect that equally strong counter pressure has to be generated through embouchure tension and closing up the larynx area. It goes without saying that unstrained and cultivated tone production is thus impossible.

② Raised shoulders

The shoulder region is the link connecting the head (including the embouchure) with the trunk (the breathing centre). Playing with raised shoulders hinders natural breathing considerably as the lungs are drawn into the upper ribcage where it becomes narrower, the arms are blocked and with them, so is the chance of playing with an organic and supple finger technique; also, usually without noticing, the player is constricting and impeding the entire tone production area including the throat and lower jaw. Likewise, raising only one shoulder (in the case of clarinettists this is usually the left one) leads to the same problems.

der die Haltung korrigieren, indem der Schüler die Arme locker am Körper herabhängen lässt. Beim erneuten Ansetzen des Instruments soll und darf sich dann der Schulterbereich nicht wieder heben.

Ein weiterer Atemfehler besteht darin, dass viel zu wenig auf eine gute **Ausatmung** in den Pausen geachtet wird. In den meisten Fällen hat man beim Spielen der Klarinette nicht zu wenig Luft, sondern eher zu viel, und man nimmt sich nicht die Zeit, die nicht zum Spielen benötigte Luft wieder auszuatmen. (Besonders sehr leichte Blätter können dann auch ausgesprochen anstrengend sein!) Gegenüber einer normalen Atmung ist also vor allem der Atemrhythmus völlig verändert. Wenn der Schüler lernen soll, vor dem Einatmen nach Möglichkeit erst die Restluft wieder auszuatmen, setzt dies eine Lockerheit und Entspanntheit voraus, die von Beginn an Ziel einer jeden bläserischen Ausbildung sein muss.

Im Zusammenhang mit der Atmung steht die **Atemstütze.** Die Atemstütze des Bläsers hat drei Hauptaufgaben: Erstens stabilisiert sie durch die Rumpfmuskulatur die Körperhaltung, besonders dann, wenn der Körper durch die Abgabe einer großen Menge Luft an Spannung verliert, zweitens sorgt sie für die Kontrolle und die Gleichmäßigkeit der Luftabgabe, was besonders bei sehr langen, sehr leisen oder sehr hohen Tönen elementar wichtig ist und drittens bewirkt die Stütze im gefühlvollen Zusammenwirken von Zwerchfell, Rumpfmuskulatur und Zwischenrippenmuskeln auf der einen Seite und Ansatzspannung und Kehlkopföffnung auf der anderen Seite für den optimalen Luftdruck beim Spielen des Instruments. Gerade bei diesem letzten Punkt werden aber immer noch aus Unkenntnis die meisten Fehler gemacht. Ein starkes Pressen im Bauchraum (gleichgültig ob nach innen oder nach aussen), ein Vorstrecken des Bauches (siehe bei „Hohlkreuz") und ein allgemeines Versteifen der Bauchdecke haben nichts mit „guter Stütze" zu tun, führen zu erheblich zu großem Druck und vor allem fatalerweise dazu, dass dann durch die Ansatzspannung und den Verschluss des Kehlbereichs ein genauso starker Gegendruck aufgebaut werden muss. Logischerweise ist dann eine lockere, differenzierte Klanggestaltung unmöglich.

② Hoch gezogene Schulter

Der Schulterbereich ist das Bindeglied zwischen Kopf (auch Ansatz) und Bauch (dem Atemzentrum). Wer die Schultern hochzieht, beeinträchtigt ganz erheblich eine natürliche Atmung, weil er die Lungen in den engen Brustkorb zieht, er blockiert die Arme und damit auch eine organische, entspannte Fingertechnik und er verengt und behindert, meist ohne es zu merken, den gesamten Bereich der Klangerzeugung mit Halsraum und Unterkiefer. Auch das Hochziehen von nur einer Schulter (bei Klarinettisten meist der linken) führt zu den gleichen Problemen.

3 Hollow back

A hollow back generally occurs as a result of the attempt to stand upright and to breathe "well into the trunk". But this should not mean causing the trunk to be protruded and hardened. As the most important "motor" of breathing, the diaphragm should drop downwards and on no account tilt forward. A protruded abdomen is therefore not a sign of good breathing. A better indication is the extension of the entire trunk, with the extending taking place sideways into the flanks. Only then is breathing support that is flexible and adjusted to suit the circumstances (see under "Breathing") possible. A hollow back can best be corrected by adjusting the head position, since together with the hollow back posture, we generally also find the:

4 Swan neck

The marked protrusion of the head and neck is known as a "swan neck". This brings with it numerous negative aspects. First of all, the holding up of the head, which is relatively heavy, requires considerable muscle work, above all in the neck region, thus causing it to be very tense. Furthermore, free and open movement of the whole neck region, even as far as the embouchure, is prevented. It is generally possible to cure a swan neck by standing erectly and bringing the instrument up to the mouth instead of holding the clarinet (out of fear?) at a considerable distance away from the body, and then stretching out the head to meet the instrument.

5 Tucking in the head

This mistake creeps in when the player's overall posture is very poor or if he or she is trying to play from music on a stand that is too low. Tall people are predestined for this error, therefore, but so are those with poor eyesight. Tilting the head downwards by only a few degrees greatly tightens the area of the larynx crucial for sound production (being directly involved with breathing in coordination with the diaphragm), affects the throat area similarly, and reduces the manoeuvrability of the tongue. The best way of countering the mistake is to look straight ahead when playing and so it can be very useful to play as much as possible by heart.

6 Position of legs and pelvis

Nowadays, many pupils have great difficulty in simply standing "normally". They either lack inner tension (which is not to be confused with being relaxed!), they put all their weight on one leg and hence, with their lopsided and unbalanced posture, have no chance of breathing well, or they tense up in an attempt "to give it their best", stand with both legs straightened and stiff, push the pelvis forward, and are in principle tensed up from top to toe. Organic posture can only be achieved by distributing the weight on both feet, which should be somewhat apart with one slightly in front of the other. The knee joints should not be artificially straightened but should provide the body with an elastic cushioning support. In this way the body remains supple and flexible despite retaining its fundamental tension. If the player is very stiff, taking a stroll around the room can be helpful.

3 Hohlkreuz

Das Hohlkreuz entsteht meist in dem Bestreben, aufrecht zu stehen und „gut in den Bauch zu atmen". „Gut in den Bauch atmen" bedeutet aber in keinem Fall ein Herausdrücken und Verfestigen des Bauches. Das Zwerchfell als wichtigster „Motor" der Atmung soll sich von oben nach unten bewegen und keinesfalls schräg nach vorn. Eine gute Atmung erkennt man also nicht am vorgestreckten Bauch, sondern an einer Erweiterung des gesamten Rumpfes, wobei sich der Körper dann vor allem seitlich und in den Flanken dehnt. Nur dann ist eine flexible, den Umständen angepasste Atemstütze möglich (siehe bei „Atmung"). Ein Hohlkreuz korrigiert man am besten durch die Stellung des Kopfes, denn meist beobachten wir in Hohlkreuzstellung gleichzeitig auch den:

4 Schwanenhals

Ein deutliches Vorstrecken des Kopfes und des Halses bezeichnet man als „Schwanenhals". Hier treten viele negative Aspekte auf. Zunächst braucht man in diesem Fall allein zum Halten des relativ schweren Kopfes erhebliche Muskelarbeit vor allem im Nackenbereich, der dann auch meist sehr verspannt ist. Desweiteren ist der gesamte Halsbereich bis hin zum bläserischen Ansatz in einer lockeren, offenen Bewegung behindert. Meist kann man einen Schwanenhals korrigieren, indem man gerade und aufrecht steht und dann das Instrument zum Mund führt, anstatt die Klarinette (aus Angst?) weit von sich zu halten, und dann den Kopf zum Instrument zu strecken.

5 Einknicken des Kopfes

Dieser Fehler schleicht sich ein, wenn die allgemeine Haltung sehr schlecht ist, oder aber, wenn man bemüht ist, Noten von einem zu niedrigen Pult zu spielen. Große Menschen sind daher für diesen Fehler prädestiniert, aber auch Menschen, die schlecht sehen können. Ein Senken des Kopfes schon von wenigen Graden verengt aber in großem Ausmaß den für die Klangerzeugung entscheidenden Bereich des Kehlkopfs, (der bei der Atemsteuerung in direkter Beziehung zum Zwerchfell steht), sowie den Bereich des Rachens und schränkt die Bewegungsfähigkeit der Zunge ein. Dem Fehler wirkt man am besten durch eine nach vorne/geradeaus gerichtete Blickrichtung. Es kann dabei sehr vorteilhaft sein, wenn so viel wie möglich auswendig gespielt wird.

6 Beinstellung und Beckenhaltung

In der heutigen Zeit haben viele Schüler schon große Schwierigkeiten damit, „normal" zu stehen. Entweder, sie sind spannungslos (nicht zu verwechseln mit locker!), belasten nur ein Bein und haben dadurch mit völlig verkrümmter und verschobener Körperhaltung keine Chance auf eine gute Atmung, oder aber sie versteifen sich im Bestreben, sich „Mühe zu geben", drücken beide Beine durch, schieben das Becken vor, und sind im Prinzip von oben bis unten verspannt. Eine organische Haltung erreicht man mit guter Gewichtsverteilung auf beide Füße, wobei diese etwas auseinanderstehen und der eine etwas nach vorne versetzt sein sollte. Die Knie sind dabei

⑦ Tense upper arms

The upper arms should be held neither at a far distance from the body nor pressed against it, an error which usually occurs in close association with the raising of the shoulders. The elbow region should be free and supple at all times. If problems are encountered in this department, doing relaxation exercises for the arms is advisable. In order to avoid tenseness from the outset, on no account should children and young people play on instruments that are too large and heavy. In the event of persistent problems caused through the weight of the instrument, an elastic neck sling may be used; this reduces considerably the pressure on the hands and arms.

⑧ Hands and wrists

There should be no kink between the hand and the lower arm as this seriously restricts the flexible movement of the fingers. The position arrived at when letting one's arms and hands hang loosely at one's side is precisely that which should be maintained when playing the instrument. Many clarinettists, however, allow their position vis-à-vis the instrument to be determined by their forefingers. In an attempt to reach the a♭ key comfortably with the left forefinger and the e♭ key with the right, they end up with a diagonal hand position that makes it extremely difficult for the little fingers of both hands to reach their keys. This means that the little fingers have to function mainly at full stretch, thereby being denied the chance of operating in a round and smoothly flowing process of movement. This almost invariably blocks the manoeuvrability of the fourth finger, too. To avoid this problem, it is far better to let the little fingers determine the playing position, as is possible on all good clarinets. The other fingers would not then lie diagonally to the tone holes but almost at right angles to them, and the movements of the third, fourth and fifth fingers would be far slighter and more comfortable, as the fingers would then be rounder and more flexible. Finding this hand position becomes easier if one imagines fingering more „into the instrument" (see illustrations 1 and 2).

¹⁾ ungünstige Handhaltung
¹⁾ adverse hand position

nicht durchgedrückt, sondern federn den Körper elastisch ab. Daher bleibt der Körper trotz einer Grundspannung biegsam und flexibel. Bei besonders verspannten Schülern kann es von Vorteil sein, sie ein wenig im Raum spazieren zu lassen.

⑦ Verspannte Oberarme

Die Oberarme sollen weder sehr weit vom Körper wegstehen, noch dürfen sie an den Körper angepresst werden, ein Fehler, der meist in enger Beziehung steht zum Hochziehen der Schultern. Der Bereich der Ellenbogen muss immer locker beweglich sein. Hier sollten bei Problemen Lockerungsübungen für die Arme durchgeführt werden. Um Verspannungen von vornherein zu vermeiden, sollten Kinder und Jugendliche auf keinen Fall zu große und schwere Instrumente blasen. Bei hartnäckigen Problemen mit dem Gewicht des Instruments kann auch ein elastischer Halsriemen benutzt werden, der die Hände und Arme sehr entlastet.

⑧ Hände und Handgelenke

Zwischen Hand und Unterarm darf sich kein Knick bilden, weil dieser eine lockere Bewegung der Finger stark behindert. Genau die Haltung, die sich ergibt, wenn man Arme und Hände locker am Körper herabhängen läßt, muss beim Spielen des Instruments beibehalten werden.
Bei vielen Klarinettisten bestimmen zudem die Zeigefinger die Position der Handhaltung in Bezug auf das Instrument. Im Bestreben, mit dem linken Zeigefinger bequem die as -Klappe und mit dem rechten die es -Klappe erreichen zu können, ergibt sich eine schräge Handhaltung, die es den kleinen Fingern beider Hände ausgesprochen erschwert, an ihre Klappen zu gelangen. Die kleinen Finger müssen dann meist ganz gestreckt arbeiten und haben damit keine Chance auf einen runden, flüssigen Bewegungsablauf.

²⁾ bessere Handhaltung
²⁾ improved hand position

Fast immer ist so auch die Bewegungsfähigkeit des vierten Fingers blockiert. Es wäre, um diese Probleme zu vermeiden, erheblich besser, wenn die kleinen Finger die Spielposition bestimmen würden, was auf allen guten Klarinetten möglich ist. Dann stünden die anderen Finger nicht schräg zu den Tonlöchern, sondern nahezu rechtwinklig, und die Bewegungen für die dritten, vierten und fünften Finger wären viel kleiner und angenehmer, weil diese Finger dann auch runder und biegsamer wären. Um diese Handposition zu erreichen hilft die Vorstellung, mit den Fingern mehr „in das Instrument hinein" zu greifen (siehe Abb. 1 und 2).

(9) Stretched fingers

The slight, loose curvature of the fingers that results when standing with one's arms dangling at one's sides should be maintained when playing. A great many clarinettists finger very firmly, stretching out their fingers so that they are straight and rigid, and in doing this they rob themselves of the chance to shape their playing with ease and subtlety.

(10) Lower jaw and embouchure

The embouchure of the instrument – how it enters the mouth – is determined on the one hand by the length and properties of the reed and on the other, quite crucially, by the player's individual mouth position. It can be learnt and experienced only in practice and cannot be explained in theory. Despite this, it is important to mention one common major problem: The ideal embouchure should influence, but not hinder, the vibration of the reed. Years of experience have shown that numerous clarinettists exercise far more pressure on the reed from the lower jaw than is necessary or favourable. Playing in the high register or in pianissimo, in particular, tends to encourage this error. But on this instrument, in order to achieve a freely vibrating pianissimo and a warm-sounding high register with good intonation, a supple and unrestricted lower jaw is essential. Especially in the sound exercises, therefore, it is important to pay constant attention to keeping the tone open, with carrying power and clean, i.e. with as little extraneous reed noise as possible.

(9) Durchgedrückte Finger

Auch die leichte, lockere Krümmung der Finger bei entspannt am Körper herabhängenden Armen sollte beim Spielen des Instruments beibehalten werden. Viele Klarinettisten greifen sehr fest, drücken die Finger stark durch und bringen sich so um jede Möglichkeit von lockerer, differenzierter Gestaltung.

(10) Unterkiefer und Ansatz

Der Ansatz des Instruments an den Mund wird einmal von der Länge der Mundstücksbahn und der Beschaffenheit des Blattes bestimmt, zum anderen aber ganz wesentlich auch von der individuellen Mundstellung des Spielers. Er ist nur praktisch erlern- und erfahrbar und entzieht sich einer theoretischen Erörterung. Trotzdem sei hier auf ein weitverbreitetes Hauptproblem hingewiesen: Der ideale Ansatz soll die Schwingung des Blattes beeinflussen, aber nicht behindern. Die langjährige Erfahrung zeigt, dass sehr viele Klarinettisten mit dem Unterkiefer viel mehr Druck auf das Blatt ausüben, als nötig und gut wäre. Gerade die hohe Lage des Instruments und das Spielen im Pianissimo verleiten zu diesem Fehler. Ein frei schwingendes Pianissimo und eine warm klingende, gut stimmende Höhe auf dem Instrument verlangen aber unbedingt einen beweglichen und freien Unterkiefer. Es ist daher vor allem in den Klangübungen immer wieder darauf zu achten, dass der Klang in diesen Bereichen frei, tragfähig und sauber ist, d. h. möglichst wenig Geräuschanteile beinhaltet.

Most clarinet manuals place the emphasis primarily on the training of finger technique. Of course, it is not the intention here to suggest that for clarinet playing a well-grounded finger technique is not necessary – on the contrary: Volume II of "Clarinet Fundamentals" will deal explicitly with finger technique in systematic order. But it is frequently all too apparent that for all the "what" of finger technique, the "how" has been sadly neglected.

To put it another way: There are hosts of clarinettists who, by investing huge amounts of time and effort, have fought their way through to the most challenging works but are not in a position to bring off the simplest of slurs (e.g. in the second movement of the Mozart Concerto) in an individual and subtly discriminating way. A high price is paid if the player has not learnt from the very outset that legato is achieved, above all, by means of breath control. One has to experience at first hand the fact that fingerwork as such requires the organic perfection that comes from a relaxed overall body posture, but in spite of – or perhaps especially due to – this, it must increasingly 'take a back seat' behind breath control and tone production. For then and only then is one approaching the goal of playing with differentiation and lyricism.

That explains why this book of "Clarinet Fundamentals" opens with legato exercises employing smaller intervals arranged in systematic order. The actual fingerwork, of course, also constitutes an important aspect of these exercises, but must be developed on the basis of a good overall body posture, through the position of the hands, the arms, the shoulders etc. The exercises are organised in such a way as to start from the simplest fingerings involving one finger only, proceeding right through to the most complex combinations such as those involved in register shifts.

Be that as it may, fingering plays only the smaller role in these exercises: The pupil must really perceive them as exercises in playing legato.
Legato is created by means of the breath control, which is influenced by the complex processes of breathing and breathing support involving the entire body. Posture, embouchure formation, tonal concept, breath control and, ultimately, perfect fingering can ensure that any legato is really dense and allow even fast passages to be slurred with lightness. In the case of changes of register, high notes or loud or very soft dynamics, in particular, perfect legato can be achieved only by means of optimal tonal control via the embouchure, moulding the tone, and setting up a clean and intensive flow of air at the moment when the note changes. The player will also find out that in the matching of airflow and finger movement, finely differentiated types of legato exist. At this point, it is worth recalling the words of the great English clarinettist Jack Brymer who said:

"Legato is the art of preparation!"

In den meisten Klarinettenschulen wird überwiegend auf die Ausbildung der Fingertechnik Wert gelegt. Selbstverständlich soll hier nicht behauptet werden, eine fundierte Fingertechnik wäre bei der Klarinette nicht notwendig – ganz im Gegenteil: der zweite Band der „Basisübungen für Klarinette" wird sich explizit mit der Grifftechnik in systematischer Ordnung befassen. Aber es ist doch immer wieder festzustellen, dass bei allem „Was" der Fingertechnik das „Wie" sträflich vernachlässigt wurde.
Anders ausgedrückt: Es gibt sehr viele Klarinettisten, die sich mit großem Aufwand und Fleiß zu den schwersten Stücken vorgekämpft haben, die aber nicht in der Lage sind, einfachste Tonverbindungen (beispielsweise im zweiten Satz des Klarinettenkonzertes von Mozart) individuell und differenziert zu gestalten. Hier rächt sich, wenn man nicht von Anfang an gelernt hat, dass ein Legato in erster Linie von der Luftführung bestimmt wird. Erst wenn man an sich selbst erfahren hat, dass das reine Greifen zwar aus einer lockeren allgemeinen Körperhaltung heraus organisch perfektioniert sein muss aber trotzdem – oder vielmehr gerade deswegen – gegenüber der Atemführung und der Klanggestaltung mehr und mehr in den Hintergrund gelangt, erst dann ist man dem Ziel eines differenzierten, gesanglichen Spiels nahe.

Am Anfang dieses ersten Bandes mit „Basisübungen für Klarinette" stehen daher Legatoübungen mit kleineren Intervallen in einer systematischen Ordnung. Selbstverständlich geht es in diesen Übungen auch um das Greifen mit den Fingern, welches aber über die Stellung der Hände, der Arme, der Schultern usw. aus einer insgesamt guten Körperhaltung entwickelt werden muss. Die Übungen sind so aufgebaut, dass sie von den einfachsten Griffen für einen einzigen Finger bis hin zu den schwierigsten Griffkombinationen beispielsweise bei den Registerwechseln reichen.

Trotzdem ist das Greifen nur der kleinere Anteil an diesen Übungen: Diese Übungen müssen vom Schüler wirklich auch als Legatoübungen verstanden werden.
Ein Legato entsteht durch die Luftführung und diese wird durch die komplexen Vorgänge bei der Atmung und der Atemstütze vom gesamten Körper beeinflusst. Körperhaltung, Ansatzbildung, Klangvorstellung, bewusste Luftführung und schließlich makellose Fingertechnik können erreichen, dass jedes Legato sehr dicht ist und dass auch schnelle Tonfolgen weich gebunden werden. Gerade bei den Registerwechseln, bei hohen Tönen oder bei lauter oder sehr leiser Dynamik ermöglicht erst eine perfekte Klangkontrolle durch Ansatz und Tonformung und eine saubere, intensive Luftführung im Moment des Tonwechsels überhaupt ein einwandfreies Legato. Dabei soll zusätzlich erfahren werden, dass es in der Einheit von Luftstrom und Fingerbewegung auch sehr differenzierte Arten von Legato gibt. Es sei an dieser Stelle an ein Wort des großen englischen Klarinettisten Jack Brymer erinnert. Er sagte einmal:
„Legato ist die Kunst des Vorbereitens!"

The six exercise sections make varying demands: In sections **a** and **b** the focus is on achieving as dense and intensive a legato as possible and here triplets and quintuplets have been chosen with the specific aim of ruling out any uniform and mechanical playing. In sections **c, d** and **e**, the principal notes should be given great intensity and the grace notes played as rapidly and lightly as possible. In spite of the blowing intensity, the fingers must remain very loose and supple. Section **f** should not sound angular but softly wave-like, whilst still being rhythmically precise.

It goes without saying that sections **c, d** and **e**, in particular, are no longer possible in the case of really tricky fingering combinations, so these are not given there. Of course, anyone feeling so inclined can experiment with what might still be playable, but must beware of any tensing up!

The aim of the exercises is relaxation!

LEGATO EXERCISES: GENERAL TIPS:

✏ Special care must be given to ensuring that all parts of the exercise are played at the same tempo (metronome).

✏ Especially in the case of complex fingering combinations (such as when switching registers), listen carefully to check that no extra notes are audible below or between those intended.

✏ For monitoring purposes, the exercises may also be played in pianissimo.

✏ Where different fingering patterns are possible, all reasonable versions should be practised as alternatives.

✏ One needs to have the sound of the notes in mind before playing them. **Legato exercises are exercises in sound sensibility!**

Die sechs Teile der Übungen haben unterschiedliche Anforderungen: In Teil **a** und **b** geht es um ein möglichst dichtes, intensives Legato, wobei absichtlich Triolen und Quintolen gewählt wurden, weil jegliches gleichförmige, mechanische Spielen vermieden werden soll. Bei den Teilen **c, d** und **e** sollen die Hauptnoten sehr intensiv sein und die Vorschläge so schnell und leicht wie möglich. Trotz der Intensität des Blasens muss man also mit den Fingern sehr locker sein. Teil **f** soll nicht eckig klingen, sondern weich wie Wellen, aber im genauen Rhythmus.

Es ist klar, dass vor allem die Übungsteile **c, d** und **e** bei wirklich schwierigen Griffkombinationen nicht mehr möglich sind, sie sind dort auch nicht mehr angegeben. Wer möchte, dürfte natürlich selbstständig ausprobieren, was noch ausführbar wäre, nur hüte man sich vor jeder Verkrampfung!

Die Lockerheit ist das Ziel der Übungen!

LEGATOÜBUNGEN: GENERELLE TIPPS:

✏ Man achte unbedingt darauf, dass alle Übungsteile dasselbe Tempo haben (Metronom).

✏ Man achte vor allem bei komplizierten Griffverbindungen (wie den Wechseln zwischen zwei Registern) darauf, dass keine Unter- oder Zwischentöne hörbar sind.

✏ Zur Kontrolle können die Übungen auch einmal im Pianissimo gespielt werden.

✏ Bei Griffalternativen sollen alle sinnvollen Möglichkeiten geübt werden.

✏ Man muss sich den Klang der Töne vorher vorstellen können. **Legatoübungen sind Übungen für das Klanggefühl!**

1. LEGATO EXERCISES WITH VERY STRAIGHTFORWARD FINGERING (1 FINGER)

AIM: The aim of the legato exercises is to produce seamless note-to-note slurs. The transition from the vibration frequency of one note to that of the other should be achieved without the slightest resistance and be as dense as possible. The flow of air must not be interrupted, not even by the smallest of "gaps".

EXECUTION: Play the following exercises in an intensive mezzoforte or warm forte at tempo ♩ = 60 – 66:

1. LEGATOÜBUNGEN MIT SEHR LEICHTEN GRIFFVERBINDUNGEN (1 FINGER)

ZIEL: Ziel der Legatoübungen sind nahtlose Bindungen von Tönen. Der Übergang von der Schwingungsfrequenz des einen Tones in die des anderen soll ohne jeden Widerstand so dicht wie möglich gestaltet werden. Der Atemfluss darf also nicht unterbrochen sein, auch nicht durch kleinste „Löcher".

AUSFÜHRUNG: Folgende Übungen in einem intensiven Mezzoforte oder einem warmen Forte im Tempo ♩ = 60 bis 66 spielen:

Proceed with the legato exercises employing the following intervals:

Die Legatoübungen mit folgenden Intervallen fortsetzen:

Boehm-System:

Oehler-System:

TIPS for sections a and b of the exercises:

- The legato must be extraordinarily exciting, varied and lovely – "basking in the legato" is allowed!

- If the slur from e-f on the first quarter note feels quite different from the f-e slur on the second, the most important step on the road to differentiated playing has already been accomplished.

- The exercise should sound extremely musical. Within certain limits (and with awareness and control) some agogics (variety in accentuation) may be used in shaping the phrases.

TIPPS für die Übungsteile a und b:

- Das Legato muss unglaublich spannend, abwechslungsreich und schön sein – man darf „im Legato baden".

- Wer spürt, dass die Bindung e – f auf dem ersten Viertel sich ganz anders anfühlt, als die Bindung f – e auf dem zweiten Viertel, hat den wichtigsten Schritt zu einer differenzierten Gestaltung schon geschafft.

- Die Übung soll sehr musikalisch klingen, darf also in gewissem Rahmen auch (bewusst und kontrolliert) agogisch gestaltet sein.

TIPS for sections c, d and e of the exercises (pages 16/17):

✏ Here, the principal notes should be played with great intensity and sonority and the grace notes played as late, as fast and as lightly as possible.

✏ In spite of the intensity of the sound, and thus of the breath control, the fingers must remain very supple and relaxed. This is hard to achieve at first and calls for a good deal of practice!

TIPS for section f of the exercises:

✏ This exercise may on no account be allowed to sound angular; although the rhythm must not be distorted, the impression created should be of soft waves of sound.

✏ Here, in particular, one never fails to be amazed how different a legato can be, depending on whether the line is rising of falling.

TIPPS für die Übungsteile c, d und e (Seite 16/17):

✏ Hier sollen die Hauptnoten sehr intensiv und klangvoll sein und die Vorschläge so spät, schnell und leicht wie möglich.

✏ Trotz der Intensität des Klanges, also der Luftführung, müssen die Finger bei den schnellen Noten sehr weich und locker sein. Dies fällt am Beginn sehr schwer und bedarf einiger Übung!

TIPPS für den Übungsteil f:

✏ Diese Übung darf auf keinen Fall eckig klingen; obwohl man nicht den Rhythmus verfälschen darf, soll sich der Eindruck von weichen Wellen einstellen.

✏ Gerade hier staunt man immer wieder, wie unterschiedlich ein Legato sein kann, je nachdem, ob es aufwärts oder abwärts geht.

2. LEGATO EXERCISES WITH VERY EASY FINGERINGS (2 FINGERS)

EXECUTION: Play the following exercises in an intensive mezzoforte or warm forte at tempo ♩ = 60 – 66:

2. LEGATOÜBUNGEN MIT SEHR LEICHTEN GRIFFVERBINDUNGEN (2 FINGER)

AUSFÜHRUNG: Folgende Übungen in einem intensiven Mezzoforte oder einem warmen Forte im Tempo ♩ = 60 bis 66 spielen:

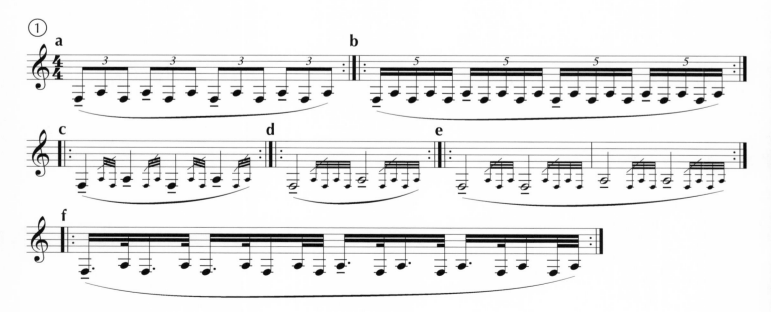

Proceed with the legato exercises employing the following intervals:

Die Legatoübungen mit folgenden Intervallen fortsetzen:

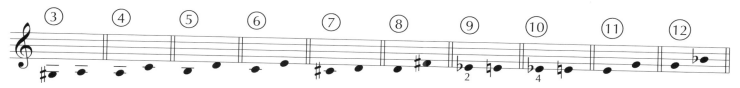

Boehm-System:

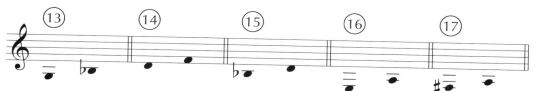

Oehler-System:

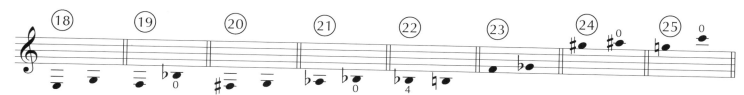

3. LEGATO EXERCISES WITH EASY FINGERINGS (3 OR 4 FINGERS)

EXECUTION: Play the following exercises in an intensive mezzoforte or warm forte at tempo ♩ = 60 – 66:

3. LEGATOÜBUNGEN MIT LEICHTEN GRIFFVERBINDUNGEN (3 ODER 4 FINGER)

AUSFÜHRUNG: Folgende Übungen in einem intensiven Mezzoforte oder einem warmen Forte im Tempo ♩ = 60 bis 66 spielen:

Proceed with the legato exercises employing the following intervals:

Die Legatoübungen mit folgenden Intervallen fortsetzen:

Boehm-System:

Oehler-System:

20

4. LEGATO EXERCISES WITH MODERATELY DIFFICULT FINGERINGS (CROSSING FROM ONE HAND TO THE OTHER)

EXECUTION: Play the following exercises in an intensive mezzoforte or warm forte at tempo ♩ = 60 – 66:

4. LEGATOÜBUNGEN MIT MITTEL-SCHWEREN GRIFFVERBINDUNGEN (FINGERWECHSEL ZWISCHEN DEN HÄNDEN)

AUSFÜHRUNG: Folgende Übungen in einem intensiven Mezzoforte oder einem warmen Forte im Tempo ♩ = 60 bis 66 spielen :

Proceed with the legato exercises employing the following intervals:

Die Legatoübungen mit folgenden Intervallen fortsetzen:

Boehm-System:

Oehler-System:

5. LEGATO EXERCISES WITH DIFFICULT FINGERINGS (a♭′, a′ AND b♭′ KEYS)

EXECUTION: Play the following exercises in an intensive mezzoforte or warm forte at tempo ♩ = 60 – 66:

5. LEGATOÜBUNGEN MIT SCHWIERIGEN GRIFFVERBINDUNGEN (as′-, a′- UND b′-KLAPPE)

AUSFÜHRUNG: Folgende Übungen in einem intensiven Mezzoforte oder einem warmen Forte im Tempo ♩ = 60 bis 66 spielen:

Proceed with the legato exercises employing the following intervals:

Die Legatoübungen mit folgenden Intervallen fortsetzen:

Oehler-System:

6. LEGATO EXERCISES WITH DIFFICULT FINGERINGS (FIRST CHANGE OF REGISTER)

EXECUTION: Play the following exercises in an intensive mezzoforte or warm forte at tempo ♩ = 60 – 66:

6. LEGATOÜBUNGEN MIT SCHWIERIGEN GRIFFVERBINDUNGEN (ERSTER REGISTERWECHSEL)

AUSFÜHRUNG: Folgende Übungen in einem intensiven Mezzoforte oder einem warmen Forte im Tempo ♩ = 60 bis 66 spielen:

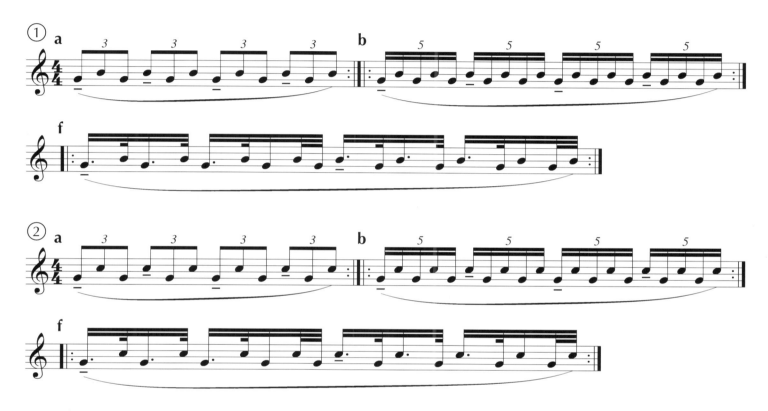

Proceed with the legato exercises employing the following intervals:

Die Legatoübungen mit folgenden Intervallen fortsetzen:

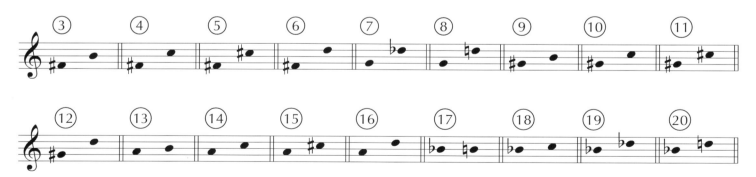

Boehm-System:

7. LEGATO EXERCISES WITH DIFFICULT FINGERINGS (HIGH REGISTER)

EXECUTION: Play the following exercises in an intensive mezzoforte or warm forte at tempo ♩ = 60 – 66:

7. LEGATOÜBUNGEN MIT SCHWIERIGEN GRIFFVERBINDUNGEN (HOHES REGISTER)

AUSFÜHRUNG: Folgende Übungen in einem intensiven Mezzoforte oder einem warmen Forte im Tempo ♩ = 60 bis 66 spielen:

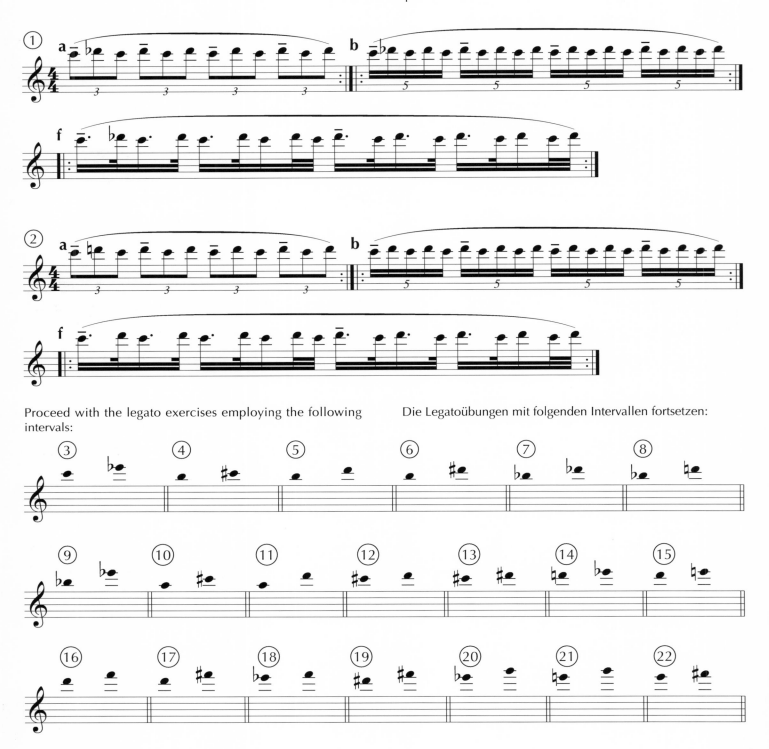

Proceed with the legato exercises employing the following intervals:

Die Legatoübungen mit folgenden Intervallen fortsetzen:

8. LEGATO EXERCISES WITH VERY DIFFICULT FINGERINGS

EXECUTION: Play the following exercises in an intensive mezzoforte or warm forte at tempo ♩ = 60 – 66:

8. LEGATOÜBUNGEN MIT SEHR SCHWIERIGEN GRIFFVERBINDUNGEN

AUSFÜHRUNG: Folgende Übungen in einem intensiven Mezzoforte oder einem warmen Forte im Tempo ♩ = 60 bis 66 spielen :

Boehm-System:

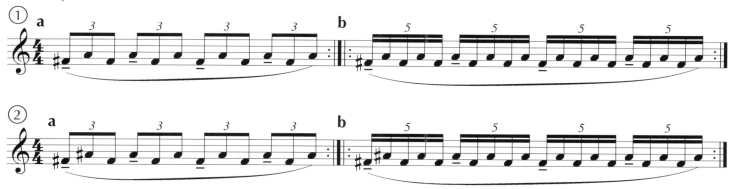

Oehler-System:

Proceed with the legato exercises employing the following intervals:

Die Legatoübungen mit folgenden Intervallen fortsetzen:

Oehler-System:

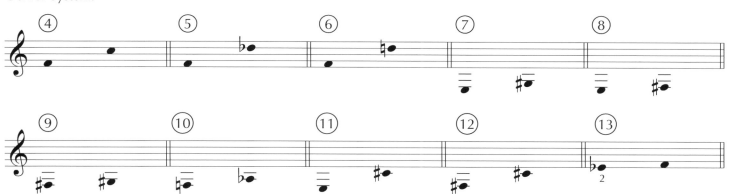

9. LEGATO EXERCISES FOR THE BASSET KEYS (BASS CLARINET, BASSET HORN, BASSET CLARINET)

EXECUTION: Play the following exercises in an intensive mezzoforte or warm forte at tempo ♩ = 60 – 66:

9. LEGATOÜBUNGEN FÜR DIE BASSETTKLAPPEN (BASSKLARINETTE, BASSETTHORN, BASSETTKLARINETTE)

AUSFÜHRUNG: Folgende Übungen in einem intensiven Mezzoforte oder einem warmen Forte im Tempo ♩ = 60 bis 66 spielen:

① *) Notated in treble and bass clef as alternatives

*) Alternativ notiert im Violin- und Bassschlüssel

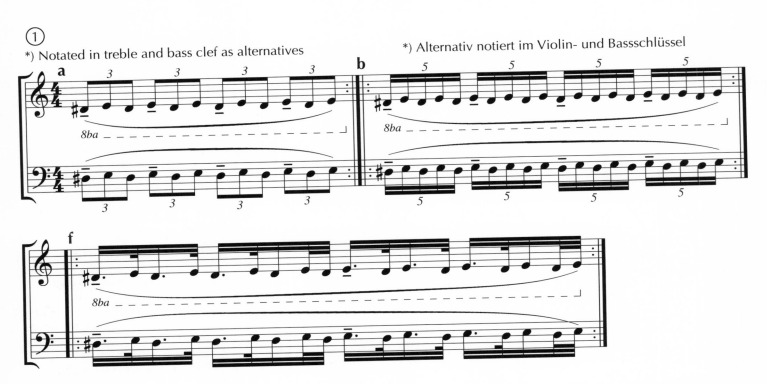

Proceed with the legato exercises employing the following intervals:

Die Legatoübungen mit folgenden Intervallen fortsetzen:

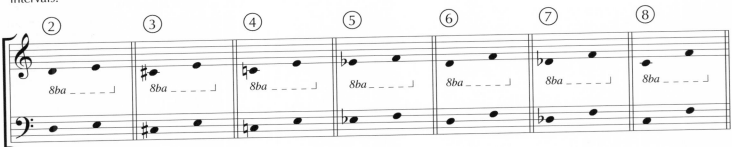

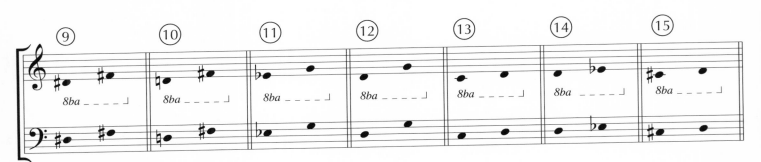

Where tone is concerned, to reach an artistic standard comparable with that of string players or singers the cultivation of tone will need to take a central place in a clarinettist's training, and a considerable part of the practice time available will have to be reserved for it. The exercises that follow are designed to trace a path through this development: no claim is laid to completeness, but the main features of all the important areas are covered. The following aspects will demonstrate to us that full tonal mastery of the clarinet is not easy!

The first aspect to be taken into consideration is purely a matter of physics: What is known to musicians as "tone" is, from the perspective of physics, a "sound" consisting of the fundamental and its overtones, which vary greatly in number. The particular tone colour results from the mixture and pronouncement – the differing strength – of these partial notes, and this mixture in turn varies enormously from player to player, from instrument to instrument and, above all, from note to note. On the clarinet, a b has a quite different spectrum of overtones to a b♭, for example. Added to this is the fact that when a note is played, the partial notes are not all formed at the same speed but in highly characteristic sequences. This phase, the "onset of vibration process", is of such crucial importance for our human hearing that despite their rather different overtone spectrum, without the onset of vibration process it would scarcely be possible for us to distinguish, for example, the flute, oboe or clarinet from one another. The mastering of the different notes' tone colour at all dynamics, as well as this onset of vibration process – i.e. the differing attack called for with each note in all registers and dynamics, therefore require extensive and systematic treatment.

On closer consideration, playing the clarinet would seem to consist of the breathing-in and the actual playing phase. But this overlooks one vital detail: Between breathing in and breathing out there is a pause or rather a phase in which the direction of the air stream is reversed. In this phase (which may be described as a "moment of repose") the air pressure needed to play the instrument is built up using the diaphragm support and the embouchure. Unfortunately, most clarinettists try to increase the pressure during this phase by closing the larynx. But this utterly rules out the possibility of clean and differentiated articulation and skilful mastery of the onset of vibration process. The highest priority of all tone exercises is thus to keep the larynx region free and open at all times and to produce the necessary (and indeed **only** the necessary) pressure using the foremost part of the tongue, as in singing the syllable "da".

Another extremely important area of tone production is perfect breath control. This means not only keeping notes stable with the help of the breathing support, even at very soft or very loud dynamics or if the amount of air taken in at a breath is close to running out. Rather, it means learning to deal with breathing organically and efficiently in general – breathing in without tightening up but with power, and breathing out with control. Furthermore, it is only possible to learn that a

Um in klanglicher Hinsicht ein künstlerisches Niveau zu erreichen, welches sich mit dem Standard bei Streichinstrumenten oder Sängern vergleichen kann, muss in der Ausbildung eines Klarinettisten die Klangschulung einen zentralen Stellenwert einnehmen und man wird auch einen großen Anteil der Übezeit dafür einplanen müssen. Die folgenden Übungen sollen dabei einen Ausbildungsgang aufzeigen, der keinen Anspruch auf Vollständigkeit erhebt, aber sicher in den Grundzügen alle wichtigen Bereiche abdeckt. Die nachfolgenden Aspekte werden uns zeigen, dass die vollständige klangliche Beherrschung der Klarinette nicht einfach ist!

Der erste Aspekt, der zu bedenken wäre, ist rein physikalischer Natur: Was der Musiker „Ton" nennt, ist physikalisch gesehen ein „Klang", der aus dem Grundton und seiner in der Anzahl sehr variierenden Obertönen besteht. Erst die Mischung und unterschiedlich starke Ausprägung dieser verschiedenen Partialtöne ergibt die spezielle Klangfarbe und diese ist wiederum von Spieler zu Spieler, von Instrument zu Instrument und vor allem von Ton zu Ton völlig verschieden. So hat z. B. bei der Klarinette ein h' ein gänzlich anderes Obertonspektrum als ein b'. Dazu kommt die Tatsache, dass sich die Partialtöne beim Anspielen eines Tones nicht alle in der gleichen Geschwindigkeit aufbauen, sondern in sehr charakteristischen Reihenfolgen. Diese „Einschwingvorgang" genannte Phase ist so wichtig für unser menschliches Hören, dass man z. B. Flöte, Oboe oder Klarinette trotz des ziemlich verschiedenen Obertonspektrums ohne den Einschwingvorgang kaum voneinander unterscheiden könnte. Die Beherrschung sowohl der Klangfarbe der verschiedenen Töne in allen Dynamikstufen als auch dieses Einschwingvorganges, also des differenzierten Anblasens von Tönen in allen Registern und Dynamikbereichen muss daher ausgiebig und systematisch erarbeitet werden.

Sieht man sich die Dinge genauer an, so besteht das Klarinettespielen aus dem Einatmen und der eigentlichen Spielphase. Doch hat man dabei ein entscheidendes Detail übersehen: Zwischen Ein- und Ausatmen gibt es eine Pause bzw. eine Phase, bei der sich ja auch die Bewegungsrichtung des Luftstromes umkehrt. In dieser (manchmal „Verhaltepause") genannten Phase wird mittels Atemstütze und Ansatz der nötige Luftdruck zum Spielen des Instruments aufgebaut. Die meisten Klarinettisten versuchen in dieser Phase leider, den Druck zu erhöhen, indem sie den Kehlkopf verschließen. Auf diese Art und Weise ist aber eine saubere und differenzierte Artikulation und eine gekonnte Beherrschung des Einschwingvorgangs völlig unmöglich. Oberstes Ziel aller Klangübungen ist es daher, den Kehlkopfbereich immer frei und offen zu halten und den notwendigen (und wirklich **nur** den notwendigen) Luftdruck (wie beim Singen mit der Tonsilbe „da") mit dem vordersten Teil der Zunge herzustellen.

Ein weiterer äußerst wichtiger Teilbereich der Klanggestaltung ist die perfekte Kontrolle der Luftführung. Dies bedeutet nicht nur, dass man mit Hilfe der Atemstütze Töne stabil halten kann, auch wenn die Dynamik sehr leise oder sehr laut ist

decrescendo calls for an increase in body tension or that a crescendo need not entail higher blowing pressure by doing appropriate exercises.

A fourth area of tonal training concerns articulation, i.e. in principle, the way in which the tongue moves in the mouth. The problem here is that in the case of the clarinet, almost all the bio-mechanical processes relevant in the tonal context take place within the body and are thus largely out of sight. Whilst a violinist's bowing, for example, is visible for all to analyse and correct, the clarinettist's tongue position in the mouth, the complex interplay between trunk and back muscles and the embouchure and larynx in the process of achieving breathing support, or indeed the whole problem of opening the larynx and keeping it unhindered, are hard for the pupil to control consciously and, for the teacher, recognisable at best by the tonal result. But without a good command of these inter-relations, acceptable articulation will never become possible and so in this crucial point, it is essential that firstly, all the processes of clarinet playing are truly understood (specialist literature!), that tone studies are played patiently and without tensing up, but also purposefully and systematically, and that through working at them on an ongoing basis, the player's consciousness and ear are trained into the bargain! **Sound exercises are exercises in conscious listening!**

The significance of a really good clarinet reed as the mediator between our artistic ideas and reality will be shown in the chapter "The Clarinet Reed". This section, therefore, will be rounded off with a final but highly significant aspect: Many of the problems associated with breathing, the larynx area and the mouth muscles are also to a considerable extent subject to psychological influences. It is no coincidence that there are sayings such as "the words stuck in his throat" or "the smile froze on his lips". In this context, when practising the whole spectrum of sound exercises what counts is learning to steer all the relevant processes as consciously as possible. Only by doing so can the proportion of unconscious processes be kept to the minimum in performance. After experiencing this over the years, playing special sound exercises immediately before public appearances then also has a distinctly relaxing and calming effect!

oder sich die eingeatmete Luftmenge dem Ende zuneigt. Es bedeutet vielmehr, dass man generell lernt, mit der Atmung – lockerer, aber kraftvoller Einatmung und gestalteter Ausatmung – organisch und effizient umzugehen. Dass darüber hinaus ein Decrescendo eine Erhöhung der Körperspannung erfordert oder ein Crescendo nicht zu höherem Blasdruck führen muss, kann man nur an geeigneten Übungen erlernen.

Ein vierter Bereich der Klangschulung betrifft die Artikulation, d. h. im Prinzip die Art und Weise, wie sich die Zunge im Mundraum bewegt. Hier haben wir natürlich die Schwierigkeit, dass sich fast alle klangrelevanten biomechanischen Vorgänge beim Klarinettespielen im Körper abspielen und daher für das menschliche Auge weitgehend unsichtbar sind. Während man z. B. bei einem Geiger die Bogenführung für jeden sichtbar analysieren und korrigieren kann, sind die Zungenstellung im Mundraum, das komplizierte Zusammenspiel von Bauch- und Rückenmuskulatur und Ansatz und Kehlkopf beim Vorgang der Atemstütze oder überhaupt die gesamte Problematik der Öffnung und Lockerheit des Kehlkopf- und Rachenbereichs für den Schüler schwer bewusst steuerbar und für den Lehrer allenfalls am klanglichen Ergebnis ablesbar. Aber ohne eine gekonnte Beherrschung dieser Zusammenhänge wird man nie akzeptabel artikulieren können, und daher gilt für diesen essentiellen Punkt, dass man erstens die kompletten Vorgänge beim Klarinettespielen auch wirklich geistig verstehen muss (Fachliteratur!), dass man geduldig und locker, aber zielstrebig und systematisch Klangstudien betreibt und dass man durch die kontinuierliche Arbeit vor allem auch sein Bewusstsein und sein Ohr schult! **Klangstudien sind Übungen für das bewusste Hören!**

Über die Bedeutung eines wirklich guten Klarinettenblattes als Mittler zwischen unseren künstlerischen Vorstellungen und der Wirklichkeit wird im Kapitel „Über das Blatt" hingewiesen werden. Zum Schluss daher nur noch ein letzter, aber sehr wichtiger Aspekt: Viele der mit der Atmung, mit dem Kehlkopfbereich und mit der Mundmuskulatur zusammenhängenden Probleme sind sehr stark auch psychisch beeinflusst. Es heißt z. B. nicht umsonst: „Die Angst schnürt die Kehle zu" oder „es gefriert das Lächeln auf den Lippen". Wichtig ist in diesem Zusammenhang, dass man beim Üben sämtlicher Klangstudien alle relevanten Vorgänge so gut wie möglich bewusst zu steuern lernt. Nur dann hat man die Chance, in Vorspielsituationen den Anteil an unbewussten Abläufen so klein wie möglich zu halten. Nach langjähriger Erfahrung sind dann spezielle Klangstudien unmittelbar vor öffentlichen Auftritten auch ausgesprochen entspannend und beruhigend!

SOUND EXERCISES: GENERAL TIPS:

- Care should be given to keeping the body relaxed overall. Even with a big and intensive sound or in extreme pianissimo, the body and, most importantly, the shoulders, must stay relaxed.

- All the exercises have a specifically prescribed tempo and so it is best to practise as far as possible using a metronome.

- The practice should not be ruled by a rigid scheme; rather, every bar should be repeated as often as is necessary.

- Very particular attention must be paid to breathing in, which is always an intrinsically important element of each exercise in line with the respective tempo.

- Every piano should embody warmth and fullness and every forte maximum volume without harshness. Although extremely quiet, the pianissimo should be free and intensive. In forte and pianissimo, one should be testing out limits rather than conserving one's strength. This increases the effectiveness of the exercises.

- If possible, sound exercises should be practised in different rooms with varying acoustics, including rooms where the acoustics are dry. This heightens the learning impact considerably.

- "Good" reeds are needed for the sound exercises, i.e. reeds that do not hiss in pianissimo and produce a warm sound with 'short' fingerings and in the upper register in forte. It will soon become clear that reeds fulfilling both these criteria are fairly rare, but if high standards are to be met, compromises should be avoided. If sound exercises are practised regularly, as a result of the improved embouchure control one soon gets the impression of having far more "good" reeds.

- Each note on the clarinet has its own characteristics of response and timbre. Some notes are "narrow" and "stuffy", and there are also notes with alternative fingerings which, as a result, can be played with different tone colouring. This becomes especially evident in exercises on response and articulation. Of course, we must attempt to improve the "poorer" notes as far as possible. To this end, it is necessary above all else to cultivate a reliable feeling for each individual note as to how it will feel and how we need to mould it. Precisely this is one of the main functions of the sound exercises.

- **Sound exercises should never be practised for too long at a time!** If one can no longer play them with full attention or enjoyment, their point is lost. The best strategy is to include them at intervals within the daily practice quota.

- **Sound exercises are "feel good exercises".** If the player feels no more relaxed after playing the exercise than beforehand, he or she has not yet got it right.

KLANGSTUDIEN, GENERELLE TIPPS:

- Man achte sehr auf allgemeine körperliche Lockerheit. Auch bei großem und intensivem Ton und auch im äußersten Pianissimo muss der Körper und vor allem der Schulterbereich locker sein.

- Alle Übungen haben ein festgelegtes Tempo, man übe daher nach Möglichkeit mit Metronom.

- Man übe nicht nach einem starren Schema, sondern wiederhole jeden Takt so oft wie nötig.

- Ganz besondere Beachtung widme man dem Einatmen, welches immer harmonisch im jeweiligen Tempo wichtiger Teil jeder Übung ist.

- Jedes Piano soll Wärme und Fülle haben, jedes Forte maximales Volumen ohne Schärfe. Das Pianissimo soll zwar sehr leise sein, aber frei und intensiv. Man achte darauf, dass man sich im Forte und im Pianissimo nicht schont, sondern Grenzen auslotet. Die Übungen sind dann effektiver.

- Wenn es möglich ist, sollte man Klangstudien in verschiedenen Räumen mit unterschiedlicher Akustik üben. Es sollten auch Räume mit trockener Akustik dabei sein. Der Lerneffekt ist dann viel größer.

- Für die Klangübungen braucht man „gute" Blätter, d. h. Blätter, die im Pianissimo nicht rauschen und die im Forte bei den kurzen Griffen und in der hohen Lage über warmes Volumen verfügen. Man wird schnell feststellen, dass es nicht so viele Blätter gibt, die beide Kriterien erfüllen, aber man sollte sich, um hohen Maßstäben zu genügen, auf keine Kompromisse einlassen. Wenn man regelmäßig Tonübungen macht, hat man durch die verbesserte Ansatzkontrolle aber auch bald das Gefühl, viel mehr „gute" Blätter zu haben.

- Jeder Ton auf der Klarinette hat seine eigene Ansprache- und Klangcharakteristik. Es gibt Töne die „eng" und „verstopft" sind und es gibt auch Töne, die man unterschiedlich greifen und damit auch unterschiedlich färben kann. Dies merkt man vor allem bei Anblas- und Artikulationsübungen. Natürlich müssen wir versuchen, die „schlechteren" Töne so gut wie möglich zu verbessern. Vor allem ist es dazu notwendig, dass wir für jeden einzelnen Ton ein ganz sicheres Gespür bekommen, wie er sich anfühlen wird und wie wir ihn zu formen haben. Gerade das ist eine Hauptaufgabe der Klangstudien.

- **Klangstudien sollte man nie zu lange üben!** Wenn man nicht mehr mit Aufmerksamkeit und Freude dabei ist, geht der Sinn verloren. Am besten verteilt man Klangstudien in Intervallen über das tägliche Übepensum.

- **Klangstudien sind „Wohlfühlübungen".** Wer sich nach den Übungen nicht entspannter fühlt als vorher, hat es noch nicht richtig gemacht.

1. RESPONSE EXERCISE

AIM: The aim of all response exercises is to achieve a clean, controlled and differentiated attack in all registers and dynamics. Mastering exercises nos. 1 and 4 (and later 15 and 21) is the precondition for tackling exercises no. 8 and 12 (and later 18 and 26). The exercises no. 30, 33, 36 and 39 come last.

EXECUTION: Play the following exercise at tempo ♩ = 60:

1. ANBLASÜBUNG

ZIEL: Ziel aller Anblasübungen ist es, in jeder Lage und jeder Dynamik Töne sauber, kontrolliert und differenziert anblasen zu können. Die Beherrschung der Übungen Nr. 1, 4 (später dann 15 und 21) ist dabei Vorraussetzung für die Übungen Nr. 8, 12 (später dann 18 und 26). Am Ende stehen die Übungen Nr. 30, 33, 36 und 39.

AUSFÜHRUNG: Folgende Übung im Tempo ♩ = 60 spielen:

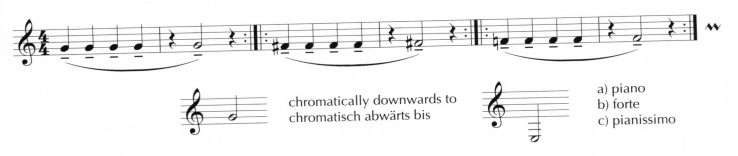

chromatically downwards to
chromatisch abwärts bis

a) piano
b) forte
c) pianissimo

The exercise should be played with great precision but also very soft attack. The tonguing should be carried out on the syllable "da". The throat cavity (larynx region) must be open even before the first note is played and also during the quarter note rests, as if breathing in easily and silently through the mouth. The entire exercise takes place "on one stream of air". The articulation effected by the tongue should not disturb or interrupt the air stream and breathing support so that the impression is not of individual notes sounding but a line of notes. In order to achieve this, only as much of the tongue as is absolutely necessary should be involved, in other words only its tip should move, not the rear part, for it is this that narrows the throat region. By listening carefully to the third and fourth notes – which in general can be played with a much lighter and softer attack than the first note or the half note – one can try to bring the more difficult notes more closely in line with the others by means of greater relaxation and openness. It is also a good idea to try singing the exercise and then to transfer the insights gained from this to playing the instrument. The exercise is easiest to play in piano and, due to the larger quantity of air involved, at its most difficult in forte.

Die Übung soll sehr präzise, aber auch sehr weich ausgeführt werden. Der Zungenstoß soll mit der Silbe „da" erfolgen. Der Halsraum (Kehlkopfbereich) muss schon vor dem ersten Ton und auch in den Viertel-Pausen offen sein, etwa so, wie beim entspannten, geräuschlosen Einatmen durch den Mund. Die ganze Übung findet sozusagen auf einem Luftstrom statt. Die Artikulation, welche durch die Zunge bewirkt wird, soll den Luftstrom und die Atemstütze nicht stören oder unterbrechen, sodass man auch keine Einzeltöne empfindet, sondern eine Linie von Tönen. Dazu ist es notwendig, dass man von der Zunge nur soviel bewegt, wie unbedingt nötig, also nur die Zungenspitze und nicht den hinteren Teil der Zunge, weil der es ist, der den Kehlkopfbereich verengt. Man achte auf den dritten und vierten Ton, die im allgemeinen viel leichter und weicher zu spielen sind, als der erste Ton oder die Halbe-Note. Man versuche, die schwierigeren Töne durch mehr Lockerheit und Offenheit den anderen Tönen anzugleichen. Außerdem ist es ratsam, diese Übung auch einmal zu singen und die dabei gewonnenen Erkenntnisse auf das Instrument zu übertragen. Die Übung ist im Piano am leichtesten, im Forte durch die größere Luftmenge am schwierigsten.

TIPS :

☞ It is crucial to ensure that after breathing in and prior to playing the first note, the pressure built up is only that required for blowing – and no more.

☞ Breathing in, "moment of repose", and start of the note should be experienced as one unit. The more harmoniously this process takes place, the smaller the problems.

☞ Remember to stay relaxed throughout.

☞ Every note must end freely and openly, not sounding dull or muted. The better the ending of each note, the easier the attack for the next.

☞ By practising in front of a mirror one can keep a good eye on one's larynx region. Ideally, no movement should be visible.

TIPPS:

☞ Man achte unbedingt darauf, dass nach dem Einatmen vor dem ersten Ton nicht mehr Druck aufgebaut wird, als zum Blasen wirklich nötig ist.

☞ Einatmen, Verhaltepause und Tonbeginn sollen als Einheit empfunden werden. Je harmonischer dieser Ablauf stattfindet, desto geringer sind die Probleme.

☞ Immer an die Lockerheit denken.

☞ Jeder Ton muss unbedingt frei und offen enden und nicht stumpf und gedämpft. Je schöner der einzelne Ton endet, desto leichter lässt sich der nächste Ton anblasen.

☞ Wenn man vor dem Spiegel übt, kann man den Kehlkopfbereich gut beobachten. Im Idealfall sollen hier keine Bewegungen zu beobachten sein.

2. ARTICULATION EXERCISE

AIM: This exercise is the "kernel" of any clean and differentiated articulation, be it portato or staccato. The exercise provides the point of departure for learning that any superfluous tongue movement is to be avoided.

EXECUTION: Play the following exercise at a calm tempo (♩ = 80):

2. ARTIKULATIONSÜBUNG

ZIEL: Diese Übung ist sozusagen die „Keimzelle" jeglicher sauberer und differenzierter Artikulation, ob Portato oder Staccato. Von dieser Übung an lernt man, mit der Zunge jeden überflüssigen Bewegungsaufwand zu vermeiden.

AUSFÜHRUNG: Folgende Übung in einem ruhigen Tempo (♩ = 80) spielen:

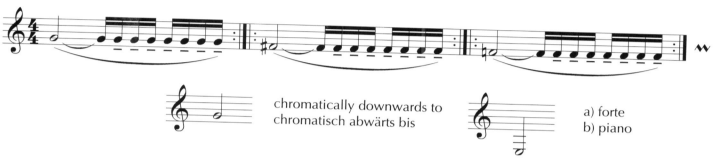

chromatically downwards to
chromatisch abwärts bis

a) forte
b) piano

Attack the note in forte and piano on a very soft "da" syllable. Then allow the note to "give" somewhat before making a slight crescendo back up to the first articulated note.

Den Ton im Forte bzw. Piano mit einer sehr weichen Tonsilbe „da" anspielen. Der Ton sollte dann etwas entspannen und zu der ersten artikulierten Note wieder leicht crescendieren.

TIPS :

- The tone quality must not be allowed to change between the sustained note and the articulated notes. If the sound in the portato section is just as good as that of the half note, all is as it should be.

- The slight crescendo to the portato is designed to prevent the player from narrowing the larynx region – and thus also the tone – during articulation, through his/her tongue movement.

- Strict attention is to be paid to moving only as much of the tongue as is absolutely necessary, i.e. the foremost part.

- As far as breath control and the throat/larynx region are concerned, one should have the feeling of sustaining the note continuously, with the tip of the tongue merely creating rhythmic interruptions to the sound flow. On no account should one have the impression of playing individual notes.

- Play this exercise before a mirror, too, and watch the larynx region.

- Always breathe at the beginning of the bar, never in the middle of the bar before the portato.

TIPPS:

- Der Klang des Tones darf sich zwischen der ausgehaltenen Note und den artikulierten Noten nicht ändern. Wenn das Portato genauso gut klingt wie die Halbe-Note, ist alles richtig.

- Das kleine Crescendo zum Portato soll verhindern, dass man beim Artikulieren durch die Zungenbewegung den Rachenraum und damit den Ton verengt.

- Es ist strikt darauf zu achten, dass sich von der Zunge nur soviel bewegt, wie unbedingt nötig, d. h. nur der vordere Teil.

- Von der Atemführung und dem Rachen/Kehlkopfbereich muss sich ein Gefühl einstellen, als ob man den Ton permanent aushält. Lediglich die Zungenspitze unterbricht rhythmisch den Tonfluß. Auf keinen Fall darf man den Eindruck haben, einzelne Töne anzuspielen.

- Auch diese Übung vor dem Spiegel üben und den Kehlkopfbereich beobachten.

- Man atme immer am Taktanfang, nie in der Taktmitte vor

3. LEGATO EXERCISE

AIM: The aim of all legato exercises is the conscious use of breath control to create the legato in both easy and more difficult slurs. This requires not only simply avoiding use of tongue articulation, but also perfectly coordinating one's idea of the sound character of the next note (especially important in the register from g upwards), breath control (especially important in the case of larger intervals) and a perfectly controlled, supple and relaxed finger technique. Some intervals can be slurred very smoothly and densely (minor sixth, minor seventh, augmented fourth) whilst others behave very sensitively (fifth, octave, major third).

EXECUTION: Play the following exercise at a calm tempo (♩ = 50) as follows:
Play the first note with a soft attack in forte (or in pianissimo, as appropriate) and sustain it. Reduce the dynamic somewhat and at the moment of the legato make a slight crescendo back to the original level. The same applies to the legato transition from the second to the third note.

3. LEGATOÜBUNG

ZIEL: Ziel aller Legatoübungen ist, dass das Legato sowohl bei leichteren als auch bei schwierigeren Tonverbindungen bewusst durch die Luftführung gestaltet wird. Dies erfordert nicht bloß simples Unterlassen von Zungenartikulation, sondern das perfekte Zusammenspiel von Tonvorstellung (besonders wichtig im Bereich aufwärts von g''), Atemführung (besonders wichtig bei größeren Intervallen) und einer vollendet kontrollierten, weichen und lockeren Fingertechnik. Es gibt Intervalle, die sich sehr weich und dicht binden lassen (Kleine Sexte, Kleine Septime, Tritonus) und Intervalle, die sehr empfindlich sind (Quinte, Oktave, Große Terz).

AUSFÜHRUNG: Folgende Tonverbindungen in einem ruhigen Tempo (♩ = 50) in folgender Art spielen:
Den ersten Ton weich im Forte (bzw. Pianissimo) anblasen und aushalten. Die Dynamik etwas zurücknehmen und dann im Moment des Legatos durch ein kleines Crescendo wieder zur ursprünglichen Dynamik zurückkehren. Gleiches gilt für das Legato vom zweiten zum dritten Ton.

a) forte
b) pianissimo

The rise and fall in dynamics is designed to support the legato but should not otherwise be obviously apparent audibly, as its purpose is to intensify the breath control. This is why it must take place at the very moment when the note changes and not shortly before. At the moment of transition from one note to the other, the impression should be of the greatest possible density. This 'legato moment' requires both great intensity of breath control and the greatest possible openness in the throat region.

Das An- und Abschwellen der Dynamik soll das Legato unterstützen und ansonsten nicht auffällig zu hören sein, es dient also der Intensivierung der Luftführung. Dafür muss es im Moment des Tonwechsels gemacht werden und nicht schon ein wenig früher. Der Moment des Übergangs von einem Ton zum anderen soll als möglichst dicht empfunden werden. Dieser Moment des Legatos benötigt dabei sowohl die größte Intensität der Luftführung als auch die größte Offenheit im Halsbereich.

TIPS :

- ✆ It is crucial that the fourth bar is observed as a full bar's rest; in so doing, the player must concentrate first on relaxing and breathing out well, before taking a big, relaxed breath in harmony with the tempo of the exercise.

- ✆ The held notes should sound tension-free (also in forte) and not be a demonstration of "power play".

- ✆ At the moment of the note change, all the intensity must be in the breath control while the remaining body regions (e.g. shoulders, arms, hands) should be loose and relaxed, especially at this point. Best results are achieved in the exercise if – despite the slow tempo – one manages to create some "swing".

- ✆ Slurring downwards across larger intervals is very hard to do. Instead of "thinking the notes down", it helps to imagine them "side by side" or to "play them forwards" – a question of visualization. Also from the physical perspective, when playing large downward slurs it helps to straighten up one's body posture.

- ✆ Even when playing forte, the finger movement must remain soft and supple.

- ✆ This exercise provides good embouchure training; it demands a great deal of energy and is well suited for warming up after a few days' break from practising, but it should not be overdone.

- ✆ Anyone feeling particularly fit can, however, extend the exercise:

TIPPS:

- ✆ Man halte unbedingt den vierten Takt voll als Pausentakt ein und achte dabei erst auf Entspannung und eine gute Ausatmung und dann auf eine große, lockere Einatmung harmonisch im Tempo der Übung.

- ✆ Die ausgehaltenen Noten sollen (auch im Forte) entspannt klingen und kein "Powerplay" darstellen.

- ✆ Im Moment des Tonwechsels liegt die gesamte Intensität in der Luftführung, alle anderen Körperbereiche (z. B. Schultern, Arme, Hände) sollen aber gerade hier locker sein. Am besten gelingt die Übung, wenn man es schafft, trotz des langsamen Tempos einen gewissen „Swing" zu erzeugen.

- ✆ Größere Intervalle nach unten zu binden ist sehr schwierig. Es hilft, wenn man die Töne nicht „nach unten" denkt, sondern „nebeneinander stellt" oder „nach vorne" spielt. Eine Frage der Vorstellung. Auch körperlich sollte man sich bei größeren Bindungen nach unten eher aufrichten.

- ✆ Auch im Forte muss man die Finger weich und locker bewegen.

- ✆ Die Übung ist ein gutes Trainig für den Ansatz, sie kostet sehr viel Kraft, sie eignet sich sehr gut zum Einspielen nach mehrtägigen Übepausen, aber man darf die Übung auch nicht übertreiben.

- ✆ Wer sich allerdings wirklich fit fühlt, kann die Übung auch erweitern:

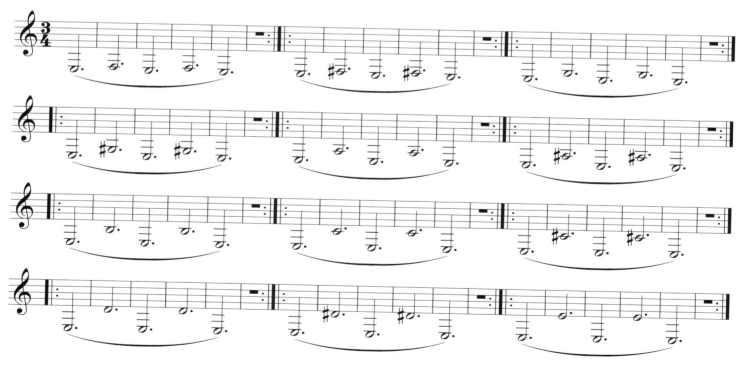

4. RESPONSE EXERCISE

AIM: It goes without saying that the same aims and tips apply to this exercise as to exercise no. 1. In contrast to the lower register, however, here one needs to pay very close attention to ensuring evenness of tone at the change of register.

EXECUTION: Play the following exercise in tempo ♩ = 60: in the same way as in no. 1:

4. ANBLASÜBUNG

ZIEL: Es gelten für diese Übung natürlich die gleichen Ziele und Tipps wie für Übung Nr. 1. Anders als in der unteren Lage muss man hier jetzt allerdings auch sehr auf die Ausgeglichenheit der Lagen beim Registerwechsel achten.

AUSFÜHRUNG: Folgende Übung im Tempo ♩ = 60 in derselben Art wie bei Nr. 1 spielen:

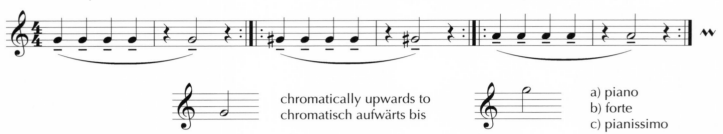

chromatically upwards to
chromatisch aufwärts bis

a) piano
b) forte
c) pianissimo

TIPS :

✏ Because of the way the clarinet is built, the notes g♯, a and b♭ sound lifeless and dull. Expressed in terms of physics, in the case of these notes the fundamental is too weak as compared to the overtones. By covering tone holes using the right hand or the little and fourth fingers of the left hand, one can (and indeed must) improve the resonance of these notes. It should not be possible for an amateur to hear any difference in tone between the registers.

✏ The point of the exercise is not only to learn about response. All the sound exercises are designed primarily for training tone! For this exercise we need a reed which allows us both to play a b♭ in a full, warm and sonorous forte as well as a b in a light, clean and effortless pianissimo!

TIPPS:

✏ Die Töne gis', a' und b' klingen durch die Bauart der Klarinette bedingt matt und stumpf. Physikalisch gesehen ist bei diesen Tönen der Grundton gegenüber den Obertönen zu schwach. Durch Abdecken von Tonlöchern mit der rechten Hand bzw. dem kleinen und dem vierten Finger der linken Hand kann (und muss) man die Resonanz dieser Töne verbessern. Ein Laie darf keinen Klangunterschied zwischen den Registern hören.

✏ Die Übung dient nicht nur dem Erlernen des Anblasens. Alle Klangübungen sollen immer vor allem den Klang schulen! Bei dieser Übung brauchen wir ein Blatt, mit dem es möglich ist, sowohl ein b' in einem vollem, warmen, großen Forte zu spielen, als auch ein h' im Pianissimo, welches leicht, sauber und mühelos ist!

5. ARTICULATION EXERCISE

AIM: The same aims and tips apply to this exercise as to exercise no. 2.

EXECUTION: Play the following exercise in tempo ♩ = 80 in the same way as in no. 2:

5. ARTIKULATIONSÜBUNG

ZIEL: Es gelten für diese Übung die gleichen Ziele und Tipps wie für Übung Nr. 2.

AUSFÜHRUNG: Folgende Übung im Tempo ♩ = 80 in derselben Art wie bei Nr. 2 spielen:

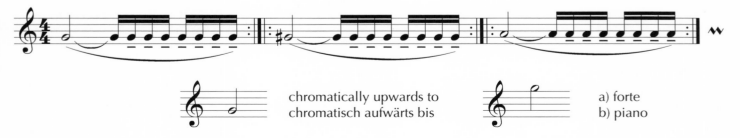

chromatically upwards to
chromatisch aufwärts bis

a) forte
b) piano

TIPS:

✏ Again, the main focus of this exercise is the perfect tonal command of the register change. The shift between b♭ and b′ requires very frequent practice both in forte and in piano.

✏ Pay careful attention that in piano the b′ speaks clearly and easily.

6. LEGATO EXERCISE

AIM: The same aims and tips apply to this exercise as to exercise no. 3.

EXECUTION: Play the following exercise in tempo ♩ = 50 in the same way as in no. 3:

TIPPS:

✏ Auch bei dieser Übung steht die perfekte klangliche Beherrschung des Registerübergangs im Vordergrund. Man übe sehr oft sowohl im Forte als auch im Piano den Wechsel zwischen b′ und h′.

✏ Man achte darauf, dass das h′ im Piano klar und leicht anspricht.

6. LEGATOÜBUNG

ZIEL: Es gelten für diese Übung die gleichen Ziele und Tipps wie für Übung Nr. 3.

AUSFÜHRUNG: Folgende Übung im Tempo ♩ = 50 in derselben Art wie bei Nr. 3 spielen:

a) forte
b) pianissimo

TIPS:

✏ On changing registers, care must be taken that no "under notes" are to be heard. If this is the case, however, try opening the register (speaker) key somewhat earlier.

✏ It is essential that the tone of the notes g♯′, a′ and b♭′ is improved by "covering" (see no. 4)

✏ When changing register, in particular, one is "trying especially hard". But the rule here, too, is: relax the shoulders, arms, hands and fingers. The key to legato lies in the breath control!

✏ This exercise may also be extended:

TIPPS:

✏ Man achte beim Registerwechsel darauf, dass keine „Untertöne" zu hören sind. Wenn das der Fall sein sollte, versuche man, etwas früher die Überblasklappe zu öffnen.

✏ Die Töne gis′, a′ und b′ müssen unbedingt durch „Abdecken" klanglich verbessert werden (siehe bei Nr. 4).

✏ Gerade beim Registerwechsel gibt man sich „viel Mühe". Aber auch hier gilt: Schultern, Arme, Hände und Finger entspannen. Der Schlüssel zum Legato liegt in der Luftführung!

✏ Auch diese Übung darf erweitert werden:

7. DYNAMICS EXERCISE

AIM: This extremely important exercise is aimed at achieving the greatest possible control of blowing pressure, without tightness or tenseness, both for attack in an unrestrained forte and also for the rapid transition to an unhindered piano. The exercise looks far easier than it is!

EXECUTION: Play the following exercise at a calm tempo (♩ = max. 50):

7. DYNAMIKÜBUNG

ZIEL: Ziel dieser sehr wichtigen Übung ist die möglichst freie und lockere Beherrschung des Blasdrucks sowohl beim Anblasen im offenen Forte als auch beim schnellen Übergang in ein unbehindertes Piano. Diese Übung sieht viel leichter aus, als sie ist!

AUSFÜHRUNG: Folgende Übung in einem ruhigen Tempo (♩ = max. 50) spielen:

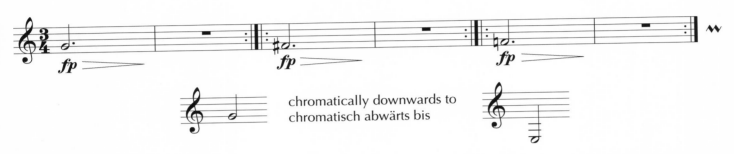

chromatically downwards to
chromatisch abwärts bis

The exercise basically consists of two parts: First, the note should be played with free and open attack in a smooth forte. One should have size in mind rather than loudness. The note should then be reduced quickly to piano and brought to a clean end. In piano, the note must sound just as "big" and free as in forte. It should not seem to require more effort, nor should it embody more extraneous noises.

Die Übung besteht im Prinzip aus zwei Teilen: Zunächst soll der Ton frei und offen im weichen Forte angespielt werden. Man denke dabei mehr an Größe als an Lautstärke. Der Ton soll dann schnell zum Piano zurückgehen und sauber ausklingen. Im Piano muss der Ton genauso „groß" und frei klingen wie im Forte. Er soll weder mühevoller sein noch mehr Geräusche beinhalten.

TIPS:

- The note should be played with a very soft attack. No explosions! Tonguing syllable "da" (not "ta").

- It is essential that the breathing in and out are without tenseness; building up excess pressure must be avoided at all costs.

- Initially, it is better to play in mezzoforte/piano, for then the beginning of the note will be louder as a result of reducing tenseness and not as a result of increasing the pressure!

- The loudest and freest point should be the beginning of the note, so there should be no subsequent pressing into it after attack!

- The forte-piano transition should feel like "gently swinging back". It is absolutely essential, therefore, that the throat region is just as open in piano as it is in forte. But "biting off" or "biting closed" the note/reed with the lips and lower jaw are also to be avoided.

- The notes should not be held too long, nor do they need to fade out "al niente".

- Singing this particular exercise every now and again yields valuable insights.

TIPPS:

- Der Ton soll sehr weich angespielt werden. Keine Explosionen! Tonsilbe „da" (nicht „ta").

- Einatmen und Anspielen müssen unbedingt entspannt erfolgen, man vermeide auf jeden Fall, einen Überdruck aufzubauen.

- Am Anfang ist es besser, ein Mezzoforte/Piano zu spielen, der Beginn des Tones wird dann dadurch lauter, dass Verkrampfungen abgebaut werden und nicht dadurch, dass man mehr drückt!

- Der lauteste und freieste Punkt soll der Beginn des Tones sein, also kein „Nachdrücken"!

- Der Übergang vom Forte ins Piano soll wie ein weiches Zurückschwingen empfunden werden. Dafür ist es absolut unerlässlich, dass man im Halsbereich im Piano so offen ist wie im Forte. Man vermeide aber auch ein „Ab-" oder „Zubeissen" des Tones/Blattes mit den Lippen und dem Unterkiefer.

- Die Töne sollen nicht zu lange gehalten werden, sie müssen auch nicht „al niente" verklingen.

- Gerade bei dieser Übung erlangt man wertvolle Erkenntnisse, wenn man sie immer wieder einmal singt.

8. RESPONSE EXERCISE

AIM: The aim is to maintain throughout the duration of rests the good feeling for response cultivated in exercise no. 1.

EXECUTION: Play the following exercise at tempo ♩ = 60:

8. ANBLASÜBUNG

ZIEL: Ziel der Übung ist, das gute Anblasgefühl aus der Übung Nr. 1 über Pausen hinweg zu erhalten.

AUSFÜHRUNG: Folgende Übung im Tempo ♩ = 60 spielen:

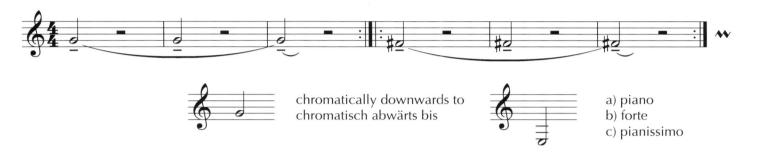

chromatically downwards to
chromatisch abwärts bis

a) piano
b) forte
c) pianissimo

TIPS:

✏ Here again, it is important that one has the feeling of playing a line of notes, not individual notes. In other words: The player's body should hold its positive tension between the notes.

✏ Taking breaths in every rest is to be avoided; take a breath only when necessary.

✏ Initially this exercise may be made slightly easier if the notes are allowed to continue sounding somewhat longer, and consequently the rests shortened.

✏ Every note must end sounding free and open, not dull or muted. The better the ending of the previous note, the easier the attack for the next.

✏ If one manages to keep up the positive body tension during the rest and the larynx region remains open (use a mirror!), it is surprisingly easy to achieve a clean response with the next note.

✏ The exercise is easier in piano and pianissimo than in forte. Should difficulties arise, therefore, it is best to work up gradually to forte via a mezzoforte.

TIPPS:

✏ Wichtig ist auch hier wieder, dass man das Gefühl hat, keine Einzeltöne zu spielen, sondern eine Linie von Tönen. Anders gesagt: Zwischen den Tönen soll im Körper die Spannung gehalten werden.

✏ Man vermeide, in jeder Pause Luft zu holen und atme nur dann, wenn es nötig ist.

✏ Am Anfang kann man sich ein wenig helfen, indem man die Töne etwas länger klingen lässt, also die Pausen verkürzt.

✏ Jeder Ton muss unbedingt frei und offen enden und nicht stumpf und gedämpft. Je schöner der Ton endet, desto leichter lässt sich der nächste Ton anblasen.

✏ Wenn man in der Pause körperlich die Spannung hält und im Kehlkopfbereich offen bleibt (Spiegel!) , lässt sich der nächste Ton erstaunlich leicht sauber anblasen.

✏ Die Übung ist im Piano und im Pianissimo leichter als im Forte, bei Schwierigkeiten sollte man sich über ein Mezzoforte an das Forte heranarbeiten.

9. ARTICULATION EXERCISE

AIM: The same aims and tips apply to this exercise as to exercise no. 2.

EXECUTION: Play this exercise in the same rhythm as no. 2 but at tempo ♩ = 100:

9. ARTIKULATIONSÜBUNG

ZIEL: Es gelten für diese Übung die gleichen Ziele und Tipps wie für Übung Nr. 2.

AUSFÜHRUNG: Im selben Rhythmus wie bei der Übung Nr. 2, aber im Tempo ♩ = 100 spielen:

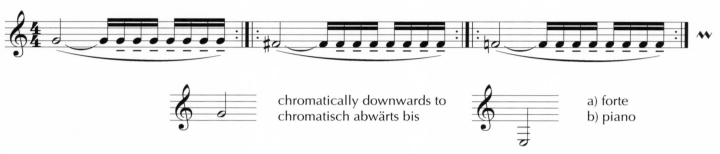

chromatically downwards to
chromatisch abwärts bis

a) forte
b) piano

TIP:

✏ Anyone who has mastered exercise no. 2 successfully might think that exercise no. 9 is superfluous, since the tempo has increased only modestly. However, as it is particularly hard to control the tone at moderate tempi, these call for particularly thorough practice!

TIPP:

✏ Wer die Übung Nr. 2 gut beherrscht, dem kann diese Übung Nr. 9 überflüssig erscheinen, weil sich das Tempo nur mäßig erhöht hat. Gerade mittlere Tempi sind aber klanglich schwierig zu kontrollieren, daher sollten diese Tempi sorgfältig geübt werden!

10. DYNAMICS EXERCISE

AIM: This is the start of a new type of exercises: All dynamics exercises are aimed at perfect command of breath control, air volume, tone colour and cleanness of sound.

EXECUTION: Play the following exercise at ♩ = 60:

10. DYNAMIKÜBUNG

ZIEL: Hier beginnt ein neuer Typ von Übungen: Alle Dynamikübungen zielen darauf ab, die Luftführung, das Luftvolumen, die Klangfarbe sowie die Sauberkeit des Klanges perfekt zu beherrschen.

AUSFÜHRUNG: Folgende Übungen im Tempo ♩ = 60 spielen:

a

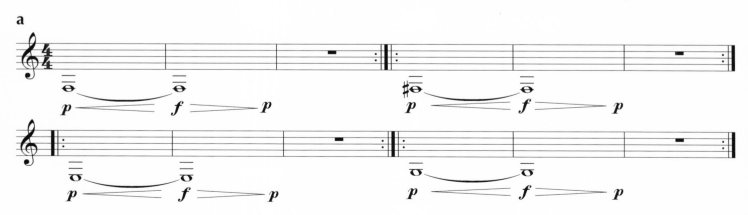

b

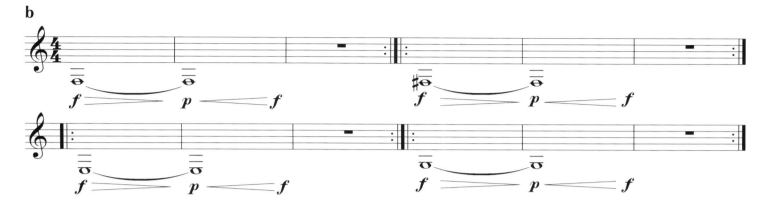

First of all, attention should be given to achieving an immaculate response (see "Response exercises"). All changes in dynamics should then be brought about by way of breath control and should not lead to any changes in the throat and lower jaw region. All transitions should be seamless. The first dynamics exercise should strike one as being really easy – the note is not very long and should not be very quiet when it starts or very loud in the middle; a single piano and single forte are sufficient. But the evenness is of prime importance! The crescendo bar and the decrescendo bar must be of exactly the same length! Avoid holding on a little longer at the end. The beginning and the ending must be exactly equal in volume!

TIPS:

✏ It makes sense to begin not with the low e but with the f, as this note is considerably cleaner, lighter and more compact both on the Boehm system and on the Oehler system.

✏ a decrescendo is not a "slackening"; on the contrary, the intensity of the breath control is increased (with breathing support). Biting the reed with the lips/lower jaw in a decrescendo is to be strictly avoided.

✏ In a crescendo, there should on no account be any forcing; the amount of air should be increased, but the air pressure raised as little as possible. If one has the feeling that the note becomes bigger "of its own accord", all is as it should be.

✏ The notes should terminate with a free and open and not a dull, stuffy sound, both in piano (in ex. **a**) and in forte (in ex. **b**).

Zunächst ist dabei auf einwandfreies Anblasen zu achten (siehe unter „Anblasübungen"). Sodann sollen sämtliche dynamischen Veränderungen von der Luftführung verursacht werden und keinerlei Veränderungen im Hals und Unterkiefer nach sich ziehen. Alle Übergänge sollen fließend sein. Diese erste Dynamikübung soll als sehr leicht empfunden werden, der Ton ist nicht sehr lang, er soll auch nicht am Anfang sehr leise oder in der Mitte sehr laut sein, ein einfaches Piano und ein einfaches Forte genügen. Ganz wichtig ist allerdings die Gleichmäßigkeit! Crescendo-Takt und Decrescendo-Takt genau gleich lang, am Schluss nicht noch ein wenig länger halten, Anfang und Ende genau gleich laut!

TIPPS:

✏ Es ist zweckmäßig, nicht mit dem tiefen e zu beginnen, sondern mit dem f, weil dieser Ton sowohl beim Boehm-System als auch beim Oehler-System viel sauberer, kompakter und leichter ist.

✏ Ein Decrescendo ist kein „Erschlaffen", ganz im Gegenteil, die Intensität der Luftführung wird erhöht (Stütze), man vermeide unbedingt, beim Decrescendo mit den Lippen/Unterkiefer auf das Blatt zu beißen.

✏ Beim Crescendo soll auf keinen Fall gedrückt werden, es soll sich die Luftmenge erhöhen, aber so wenig wie möglich der Luftdruck. Wenn man das Gefühl hat, dass der Ton „von alleine" größer wird, ist alles richtig.

✏ Die Töne sollen sowohl im Piano (bei **a**) als auch im Forte (bei **b**) offen und frei enden und nicht stumpf.

11. LEGATO EXERCISE

AIM: The same aims and tips apply to this exercise as to exercises no. 3 and 6.

EXECUTION: Play the following exercise at tempo ♩ = 50 in the same way as no. 3:

11. LEGATOÜBUNG

ZIEL: Es gelten für diese Übung die gleichen Ziele wie für die Übungen Nr. 3 und Nr. 6

AUSFÜHRUNG: Folgende Übung im Tempo ♩ = 50 in derselben Art wie bei Übung Nr. 3 spielen:

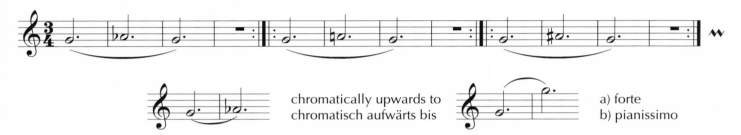

chromatically upwards to
chromatisch aufwärts bis

a) forte
b) pianissimo

TIPS:

✏ Even when having to move all fingers, such as between g und b , the slurring is done by means of the breath; the fingers simply have to play along perfectly, i.e. the finger movement must be supple and synchronised and not too quick.

✏ It will become clear that this exercise is very hard, but nevertheless one should try to avoid playing it tentatively and cautiously; **the exercise requires relaxation and courage!**

✏ Due to the combination of the short air column of the g and the "long" fingerings (b , c , c♯) the intonation in this exercise is not all that easy either and calls for special care.

✏ Likewise, this exercise may be extended:

TIPPS:

✏ Auch wenn man alle Finger bewegen muss wie zwischen g' und h', soll man mit der Luft binden. Die Finger müssen nur perfekt mitspielen, d. h., die Fingerbewegung muss weich, synchron und nicht zu schnell sein.

✏ Man wird feststellen, dass die Übung sehr schwierig ist. Trotzdem hüte man sich davor, zaghaft und vorsichtig zu sein, **die Übung braucht Lockerheit und Mut!**

✏ Durch die Kombination der kurzen Luftsäule beim g' mit den „langen" Griffen (h', c'', cis'') ist bei dieser Übung auch die Intonation nicht ganz einfach und benötigt besondere Beachtung.

✏ Auch diese Übung darf erweitert werden:

12. RESPONSE EXERCISE

AIM: The same aims and tips apply to this exercise as to exercise no. 8.

EXECUTION: Play this exercise in the same rhythm and manner as no. 8 (♩ = 60):

12. ANBLASÜBUNG

ZIEL: Es gelten für diese Übung die gleichen Ziele und Tipps wie für Übung Nr. 8.

AUSFÜHRUNG: Im selben Rhythmus und in der selben Art wie bei Nr. 8 spielen (♩ = 60)

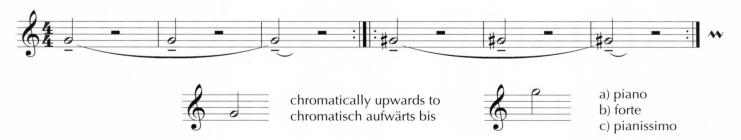

chromatically upwards to
chromatisch aufwärts bis

a) piano
b) forte
c) pianissimo

13. ARTICULATION EXERCISE

AIM: The same aims and tips apply to this exercise as to exercises no. 2, no. 5 and no. 9.

EXECUTION: Play this exercise in the same rhythm as no. 2 but at tempo ♩ = 100:

13. ARTIKULATIONSÜBUNG

ZIEL: Es gelten für diese Übung die gleichen Ziele und Tipps wie für die Übungen Nr. 2, Nr. 5 und Nr. 9.

AUSFÜHRUNG: Im selben Rhythmus wie bei der Übung Nr. 2, aber im Tempo ♩ = 100 spielen:

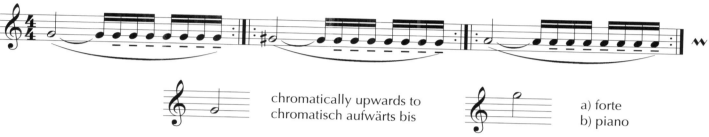

chromatically upwards to
chromatisch aufwärts bis

a) forte
b) piano

TIP:

✏ When increasing the tempo from here onwards, we must be careful to ensure that the notes b and c speak cleanly and effortlessly.

TIPP:

✏ Wenn wir von nun an das Tempo steigern, müssen wir unbedingt darauf achten, dass die Töne h' und c'' sauber und mühelos ansprechen.

14. DYNAMICS EXERCISE

AIM: The same aims and tips apply to this exercise as to exercise no. 7.

EXECUTION: Play this exercise in the same manner and tempo (♩ = max. 50) as exercise no. 7:

14. DYNAMIKÜBUNG

ZIEL: Es gelten für diese Übung die gleichen Ziele und Tipps wie für Übung Nr. 7.

AUSFÜHRUNG: In der selben Art und im selben Tempo (♩ = max. 50) wie bei Übung Nr. 7 spielen:

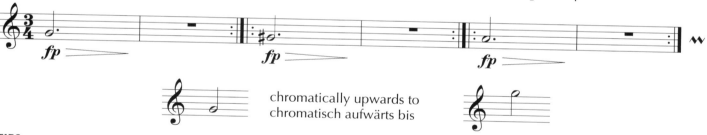

chromatically upwards to
chromatisch aufwärts bis

TIPS:

✏ Here again, as in every exercise incorporating the change of register it is advisable to play the notes b♭ and b in frequent alternation, so that these extremely dissimilar notes become more balanced and even in terms of sound.

✏ In the case of b♭ one has to take care that the forte is not "stifled" or "choked" but keeps its full resonance.

✏ In the case of b , watch that a clean, free piano is achieved directly after the forte.

✏ There are notes that sound fuller and freer and others that sound tighter (such as c♯ , f♯ , d♯ , for example); these narrower-sounding notes cannot tolerate any pressure in forte. Only when the playing is free and open can the tone be as round as that of the other notes.

TIPPS:

✏ Auch hier wieder, wie bei jeder Übung mit Registerwechsel, ist es ratsam, die Töne b' und h' oft abwechselnd zu blasen, damit diese extrem unterschiedlichen Töne klanglich angeglichen werden.

✏ Beim b' muss man aufpassen, dass das Forte nicht „abgedrückt" wird, sondern volles Volumen behält.

✏ Beim h' muss man darauf achten, dass man direkt nach dem Forte ein sauberes, freies Piano erreicht.

✏ Es gibt Töne, die voller und freier klingen, und Töne, die enger sind (wie z. B. cis" , fis" , dis"), diese engeren Töne vertragen im Forte überhaupt keinen Druck. Nur wenn man frei und offen bleibt, wird der Klang so rund wie bei den anderen Tönen.

15. RESPONSE EXERCISE

AIM: The same aims and tips apply here as to exercises no. 1 and no. 4.

EXECUTION: Play this exercise at tempo ♩ = 60:

15. ANBLASÜBUNG

ZIEL: Es gelten für diese Übung die gleichen Ziele und Tipps wie bei den Übungen Nr. 1 und Nr. 4.

AUSFÜHRUNG: Folgende Übung im Tempo ♩ = 60 spielen:

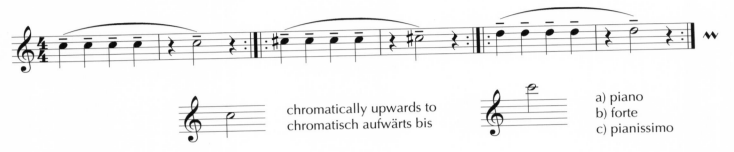

chromatically upwards to
chromatisch aufwärts bis

a) piano
b) forte
c) pianissimo

TIPS:

✎ An exercise of prime importance for attack and the shaping of tone in the clarinet's most important register.

✎ The forte should be as 'big' as possible, with high projection, and should sound brilliant, warm and full, **never strident.**

✎ The pianissimo, on the other hand, must on no account be allowed to become thinner on the high notes but **always sound free and effortless!** For this, it is important that one does not shorten the vibrating part of the reed too much with the embouchure, as this (along with errors in the throat region) narrows the tone. Even a soft high note requires a surprisingly large quantity of air!

TIPPS:

✎ Eine ausgesprochen wichtige Übung für das Anblasen und die Klanggestaltung in der wichtigsten Lage der Klarinette.

✎ Das Forte soll so groß wie möglich sein, voller Strahlkraft und leuchtend, warm und voll, also **immer ohne jede Schärfe.**

✎ Das Pianissimo dagegen darf auf keinen Fall bei den oberen Tönen enger werden, es soll **immer frei und mühelos klingen!** Dafür ist es wichtig, dass man mit dem Ansatz den schwingenden Teil des Blattes nicht zu sehr verkürzt, denn das macht (zusätzlich zu Fehlern im Halsbereich) den Ton eng. Auch ein leiser Ton in der Höhe braucht erstaunlich viel Luft!

16. LEGATO EXERCISE

AIM: The same aims and tips apply here as to exercises no. 3, no. 6 and no. 11.

EXECUTION: Play this exercise in the same manner and tempo (♩ = 50) as exercise no. 3:

16. LEGATOÜBUNG

ZIEL: Es gelten für diese Übung die gleichen Ziele und Tipps wie für die Übungen Nr. 3, Nr. 6 und Nr. 11.

AUSFÜHRUNG: In derselben Art und im selben Tempo (♩ = 50) wie bei der Übung Nr. 3 spielen:

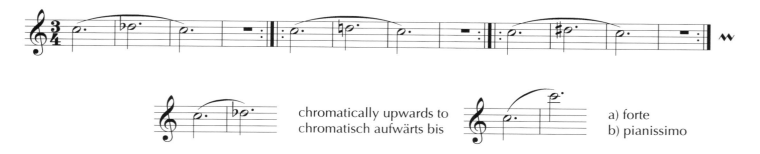

chromatically upwards to
chromatisch aufwärts bis

a) forte
b) pianissimo

TIPS:

- Again, an exercise of the utmost importance in the clarinet's "golden register"; here is the opportunity to develop a wonderful feeling for a fine legato.

- Certain intervals which are easy to finger are hard to slur from the point of view of sound (e.g. c /a), and conversely there are those that can be easily slurred soundwise but are more difficult to finger (e.g. c /a♭ or c /e♭).

- The interval c /a is highly significant since it occurs frequently. But it is hard to slur, especially upwards. It is crucial to pay special attention to the sound of the a , which should be soft and dark. On no account should one try to use power in slurring upwards. **This interval works only with a feeling for sound!** If having trouble, one should start on the a and begin by slurring downwards.

- Take great care to produce a free sound on the upper notes a , b♭ , b and c , i.e. neither forced in forte nor thin in piano.

- Extend this exercise too:

TIPPS:

- Ebenfalls eine äußerst wichtige Übung in der „goldenen Lage" der Klarinette, hier kann man ein wunderbares Gefühl für ein schönes Legato entwickeln.

- Es gibt Intervalle, die sich leicht greifen lassen, die aber klanglich schwer zu binden sind (wie z.B. c''/a''), und den umgekehrten Fall, der klanglich gut bindet, aber durch die Griffverbindung schwieriger ist (wie z. B. c''/as'' oder c''/es'').

- Das Intervall c''/a'' ist sehr wichtig, weil es oft vorkommt. Es ist aber schwierig zu binden, vor allem aufwärts. Man achte hier unbedingt auf den Klang des a'', dieser muss weich und dunkel sein. Auf keinen Fall darf man versuchen, mit Kraft nach oben zu binden. **Dieses Intervall gelingt nur mit Klanggefühl!** Bei Schwierigkeiten sollte man mit dem a'' beginnen und zuerst nach unten binden.

- Man achte unbedingt darauf, dass man bei den oberen Tönen a'', b'', h'' und c''' einen freien Klang erzeugt, nicht gepresst im Forte, nicht eng im Piano.

- Auch diese Übung erweitern:

17. DYNAMICS EXERCISE

AIM: The same aims and tips apply here as to exercise no. 10.

EXECUTION: Play the following notes in the same manner and tempo (♩ = 60) as in exercise no. 10:

17. DYNAMIKÜBUNG

ZIEL: Es gelten für diese Übung die gleichen Ziele und Tipps wie für Übung Nr. 10.

AUSFÜHRUNG: In derselben Art und im selben Tempo (♩ = 60) wie bei Übung Nr. 10 folgende Töne spielen:

TIPS:

- Once again, the point of this exercise is to achieve evenness at the awkward change of register. Volume, clean sound and lightness should be as similar as possible on the b♭ and the b .

- At this first stage in the dynamics exercises, no extreme dynamics are called for; a single piano and single forte are enough!

- In general, for the dynamics exercises it is sufficient to work through the low notes in exercise no. 10 and the change-of-register notes in this exercise, no. 17. But all other notes may also be included if wished.

TIPPS:

- Wieder geht es hier um den Ausgleich des schwierigen Registerwechsels. Volumen, klangliche Sauberkeit und Leichtigkeit sollen beim b' und beim h' so ähnlich wie möglich werden.

- Bei dieser ersten Stufe der Dynamikübungen keine extreme Dynamik, einfaches Piano und einfaches Forte reichen!

- Im allgemeinen reichen für die Dynamikübungen die tiefen Töne der Übung Nr. 10 und die Töne des Registerwechsels von dieser Übung Nr. 17. Man kann aber auch alle weiteren Töne mit einbeziehen.

18. RESPONSE EXERCISE

AIM: The same aims and tips apply here as to exercises no. 8 and no. 12.

EXECUTION: Play this exercise in the same manner and tempo (♩ = 60) as exercises no. 8 and 12:

18. ANBLASÜBUNG

ZIEL: Es gelten für diese Übung die gleichen Ziele und Tipps wie für die Übungen Nr. 8 und Nr. 12.

AUSFÜHRUNG: In derselben Art und im selben Tempo (♩ = 60) wie bei Übung Nr. 8 und Nr. 12 spielen:

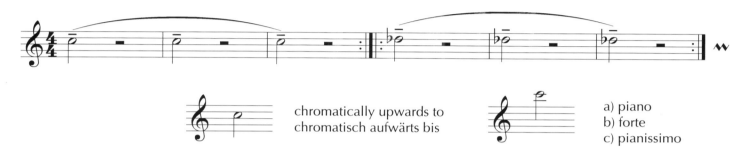

chromatically upwards to
chromatisch aufwärts bis

a) piano
b) forte
c) pianissimo

19. LEGATO EXERCISE

AIM: The same aims and tips apply here as to exercises no. 3 no. 6, no. 11 and no. 16.

EXECUTION: Play this exercise in the same manner and tempo (♩ = 50) as exercise no. 3:

19. LEGATOÜBUNG

ZIEL: Es gelten für diese Übung die gleichen Ziele und Tipps wie für die Übungen Nr. 3, Nr. 6, Nr. 11 und Nr. 16.

AUSFÜHRUNG: In derselben Art und im selben Tempo (♩ = 50) wie bei Übung Nr. 3 spielen:

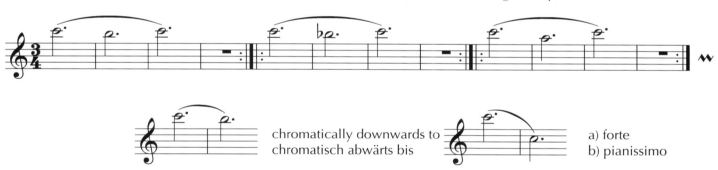

chromatically downwards to
chromatisch abwärts bis

a) forte
b) pianissimo

TIPS:

✎ The central importance of this register makes especially thorough practice a necessity, so here the legato exercise is taken from the top downwards, for once.

✎ This exercise is very tiring and, when played in forte, strengthens the embouchure. In piano the danger is that the embouchure becomes too firm. Should difficulties arise, one should take repeated breaks and practise something else!

✎ Extend this exercise too:

TIPPS:

✎ Die Wichtigkeit dieser Lage erfordert besonders gründliche Übung. Daher in dieser Lage die Legatoübung auch einmal von oben nach unten.

✎ Diese Übung ist sehr anstrengend, sie stärkt im Forte den Ansatz. Im Piano besteht die Gefahr, dass der Ansatz fest wird. Bei Schwierigkeiten sollte man zwischendurch immer Pausen machen und andere Dinge üben!

✎ Auch diese Übung erweitern:

20. DYNAMICS EXERCISE

AIM: The same aims and tips apply here as to exercises no.7 and no. 14.

EXECUTION: Play this exercise in the same manner and tempo (♩ = max. 50) as exercise no. 7:

20. DYNAMIKÜBUNG

ZIEL: Es gelten für diese Übung die gleichen Ziele und Tipps wie für die Übungen Nr. 7 und Nr. 14.

AUSFÜHRUNG: In derselben Art und im selben Tempo (♩ = max. 50) wie bei Übung Nr. 7 spielen:

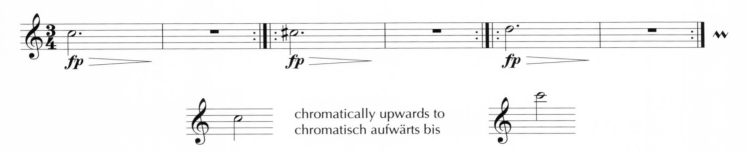

chromatically upwards to
chromatisch aufwärts bis

TIP:

✏ Here, too, especially in the case of the high notes it is best to begin with a mezzoforte/piano, since the danger of pinching the note closed becomes ever greater the higher one plays. The beginning of the note should always sound warm and dark.

TIPP:

✏ Auch hier gerade bei den höheren Tönen zuerst mit Mezzoforte/Piano beginnen, weil nach oben hin die Gefahr, den Ton abzudrücken immer größer wird. Der Tonbeginn muss immer warm und dunkel klingen.

21. RESPONSE EXERCISE

AIM: The same aims and tips apply here as to exercises no.1, no. 4 and no. 15.

EXECUTION: Play this exercise in the same rhythm and tempo (♩ = 60) as exercise no. 1:

21. ANBLASÜBUNG

ZIEL: Es gelten für diese Übung die gleichen Ziele und Tipps wie für die Übungen Nr. 1, Nr. 4 und Nr. 15.

AUSFÜHRUNG: Im Rhythmus und Tempo (♩ = 60) wie bei Übung Nr. 1 spielen:

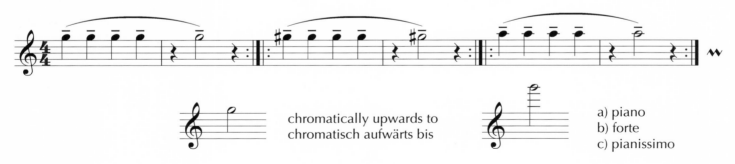

chromatically upwards to
chromatisch aufwärts bis

a) piano
b) forte
c) pianissimo

TIPS:

✏ Here we come to the next change of register. We need to practise the notes c and d♭ very frequently in alternation. Whilst the c (especially with the forked fingering of the Oehler system) requires a great deal of air (also in pianissimo!), the d♭ speaks much more easily than most clarinettists think. Not a great deal of pressure from the lower lip or lower jaw is needed for either note; the point of embouchure pressure is of greater relevance, since the vibrating portion of the reed needs to be long enough.

TIPPS:

✏ Wir kommen zum nächsten Registerwechsel. Hier müssen wir sehr oft die Töne c''' und des''' abwechselnd üben. Während das c''' (vor allem beim Gabelgriff des Oehler-Systems) sehr viel Luft braucht (auch im Pianissimo!), geht das des''' wesentlich leichter, als die meisten Klarinettisten denken. Bei beiden Tönen braucht man nicht sehr viel Druck mit der Unterlippe bzw. dem Unterkiefer, der Druckpunkt ist wichtiger, das Blatt muss in ausreichender Länge schwingen.

If one applies too much embouchure pressure when playing the high notes, very little air passes through the mouthpiece (giving a small, thin tone). In piano, especially, one then also tends to be far too sharp. However, if one monitors the intonation carefully and plays flat enough, the reduction in embouchure pressure also leads to improvements in tone and response!

It is crucial to ensure that when playing the notes in the high register one remains altogether free of stiffness in the entire body.

22. ARTICULATION EXERCISE

AIM: The same aims and tips apply here as to exercise no. 2.

EXECUTION: Play the following exercise at a calm tempo (♩ = 80):

Wenn man bei den hohen Tönen zu viel drückt, geht sehr wenig Luft durch das Mundstück (kleiner und enger Ton). Vor allem im Piano ist man dann auch meist deutlich zu hoch. Wenn man dagegen auf die Intonation achtet und tief genug spielt, verbessert sich durch die Verminderung des Ansatzdrucks auch der Klang und die Ansprache!

Es ist unbedingt darauf zu achten, dass man bei den Tönen der hohen Lage insgesamt körperlich entspannt bleibt.

22. ARTIKULATIONSÜBUNG

ZIEL: Es gelten für diese Übung die gleichen Ziele und Tipps wie für die Übung Nr. 2.

AUSFÜHRUNG: Folgende Übung in einem ruhigen Tempo (♩ = 80) spielen:

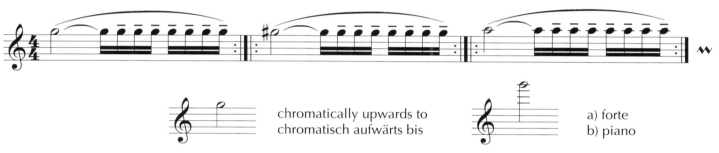

chromatically upwards to
chromatisch aufwärts bis

a) forte
b) piano

TIPS:

For the change of register, all that was noted in no. 21 applies here too.

Thanks to the previous articulation exercises, the mobility of the tongue should be well trained by now. If the tonguing is still rather clumsy, however, the note can easily 'stall' in this register.

At the same time, it is important that the tip of the tongue now makes deft contact with the reed, as otherwise the high-frequency vibration can very easily be disturbed.

TIPPS:

Für den Registerwechsel gilt alles bei Nr. 21 Gesagte.

Die Bewegungsfähigkeit der Zunge sollte durch alle vorangegangenen Artikulationsübungen nun schon gut trainiert sein. Wenn jetzt doch noch zuviel Aufwand stattfindet, reißt in dieser Lage leicht der Ton ab.

gleichzeitig muss die Zungenspitze jetzt geschickt an das Blatt stoßen, die hohe Frequenz der Schwingung wird sonst sehr leicht behindert.

23. ARTICULATION EXERCISE

AIM: The same aims and tips apply here as to previous articulation exercises.

EXECUTION: The same exercise as no. 2 but play it this time at tempo ♩ = 120:

23. ARTIKULATIONSÜBUNG

ZIEL: Es gelten bei dieser Übung die gleichen Ziele und Tipps wie für die vorangegangenen Artikulationsübungen.

AUSFÜHRUNG: Dieselbe Übung wie in Übung Nr. 2, nur diesmal im Tempo ♩ = 120 spielen:

chromatically downwards to
chromatisch abwärts bis

a) forte
b) piano

TIPS:

- As the tempo increases, it is vital to watch that one is not late starting the tonguing! Apart from the fact that this is rhythmically incorrect, one has the subjective impression that the tempo must be very fast and one needs to hurry. However in contrast, by tonguing as early as possible the tempo strikes one as being very comfortable.

- One should still be playing with a broad portato. Some clarinettists have trouble with this in the quicker tempo, in which case somewhat shorter articulation may also be used, but it is as important as ever that the tone is full and round.

TIPPS:

- Wenn sich das Tempo nun erhöht, muss man unbedingt darauf achten, dass man mit der Artikulation nicht zu spät beginnt! Abgesehen davon, dass dies rhythmisch ein Fehler ist, hat man dann subjektiv den Eindruck, dass das Tempo sehr schnell ist und man sich beeilen muss. Wenn man dagegen so früh wie möglich artikuliert, empfindet man das Tempo als sehr bequem.

- Es sollte immer noch ein breites Portato gespielt werden. Manchem Klarinettisten macht das im schnellen Tempo Mühe. Man kann dann auch etwas kürzer artikulieren. Wichtig bleibt aber der volle, runde Klang.

24. DYNAMICS EXERCISE

AIM: The same aims and tips apply here as to exercises no. 10 and no. 17.

EXECUTION: Play the following exercises at tempo ♩ = 60:

24. DYNAMIKÜBUNG

ZIEL: Es gelten bei diesen Übungen die gleichen Ziele und Tipps wie für die Übungen Nr. 10 und Nr. 17.

AUSFÜHRUNG: Folgende Übungen im Tempo ♩ = 60 spielen:

a

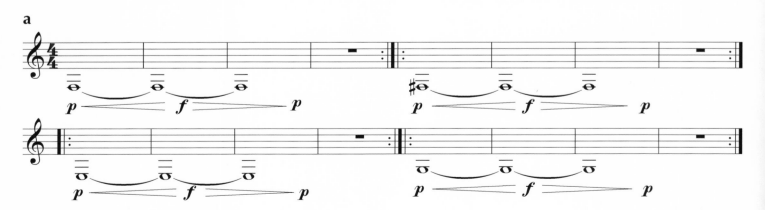

b

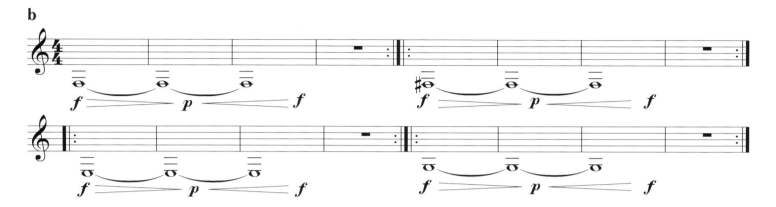

All that was stated for exercise no. 10 applies here too: The piano (or forte) should be reached precisely half-way through!	Es gilt alles bei der Übung Nr. 10 Gesagte: Das Piano (bzw. Forte) soll genau in der Mitte sein!

TIP:	**TIPP:**
✏ Again, these are not – as yet – lengthy exercises involving great dynamic contrasts. If one allows the notes to flow without pressure during the crescendo and without loss of tension during the decrescendo, the exercises will seem quite straightforward. Then one can by all means "risk" a little more at the quieter end of the dynamic scale and approach a pianissimo.	✏ Auch hier handelt es sich noch nicht um lange Übungen mit großen dynamischen Unterschieden. Wenn man die Töne ohne Druck im Crescendo und ohne Spannungsverlust im Decrescendo fließen lässt, wird man sie als ganz einfach empfinden. Dann kann man dynamisch im leisen Bereich auch ruhig etwas „riskieren" und mehr ins Pianissimo gehen.

25. ARTICULATION EXERCISE

AIM: The same aims and tips apply here as to the previous articulation exercises.

EXECUTION: The same exercise as no. 22 but play it this time at tempo ♩ = 100:

25. ARTIKULATIONSÜBUNG

ZIEL: Es gelten bei dieser Übung die gleichen Ziele und Tipps wie für die vorangegangenen Artikulationsübungen.

AUSFÜHRUNG: Die gleiche Übung wie Nr. 22, nur diesmal im Tempo ♩ = 100 spielen:

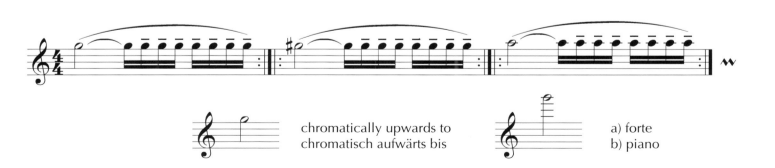

chromatically upwards to
chromatisch aufwärts bis

a) forte
b) piano

26. RESPONSE EXERCISE

AIM: The same aims and tips apply here as to all previous response exercises, especially no. 8 and no. 21.

EXECUTION: Play this exercise in the same rhythm and tempo (♩ = 60) as exercise no. 8:

26. ANBLASÜBUNG

ZIEL: Es gelten für diese Übung die gleichen Ziele und Tipps wie für alle vorangegangenen Anblasübungen vor allem Nr. 8 und Nr. 21.

AUSFÜHRUNG: Im Rhythmus und Tempo (♩ = 60) wie bei Übung Nr. 8 spielen:

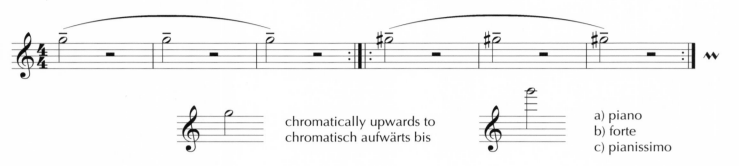

chromatically upwards to
chromatisch aufwärts bis

a) piano
b) forte
c) pianissimo

TIPS:

✆ Here, too, it makes sense to hold the notes somewhat longer at first, thereby shortening the rests.

✆ Response problems often arise in this register as a result of the larynx region closing up after all. Should these difficulties persist, the notes may – as an exception – be played by blowing them without tonguing (in particular c   / d♭   /d   ). If in the course of doing this one takes notice of how easily these notes speak when played with an open throat, one can then duplicate this feeling when playing with proper tongue attack.

TIPPS:

✆ Auch hier ist es sinnvoll, zunächst die Töne etwas zu verlängern, also die Pausen zu verkürzen.

✆ Häufig gibt es in diesem Register Schwierigkeiten beim Anblasen, weil der Kehlkopfbereich doch verengt wurde. Bei anhaltenden Schwierigkeiten ist es hier ausnahmsweise auch einmal erlaubt, die Töne (vor allem c‴/des‴/d‴) ohne Zungenstoß nur anzuhauchen. Wenn man daran bemerkt, wie leicht diese Töne bei geöffnetem Halsraum ansprechen, kann man dieses Gefühle auch auf das korrekte Anblasen mit der Zunge übertragen.

27. LEGATO EXERCISE

AIM: This is the last in the series of legato exercises, and also the most challenging. The same aims and tips apply here as for exercises no. 3, no. 6 and no. 11.

EXECUTION: Play this exercise at the same tempo (♩ = 50) as exercise no. 3:

27. LEGATOÜBUNG

ZIEL: Die letzte in der Reihe der Legatoübungen, allerdings auch die Anspruchvollste. Es gelten die gleichen Ziele und Tipps wie für die Übungen Nr. 3, Nr. 6 und Nr. 11.

AUSFÜHRUNG: In derselben Art und im selben Tempo (♩ = 50) wie bei der Übung Nr. 3 spielen:

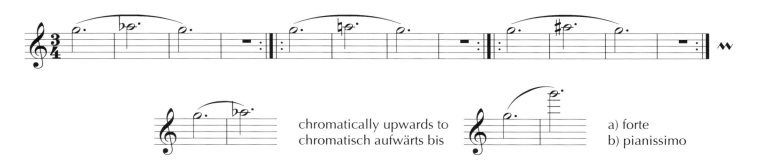

chromatically upwards to
chromatisch aufwärts bis

a) forte
b) pianissimo

TIPS:

✏ In terms of their individual characteristics, the notes in the third register vary enormously. The d♭ , e♭ ,g♭ and g speak surprisingly easily, as long they are allowed to vibrate freely and are dark in tone. They require far less air pressure than g or c , for example, and are most successful when one aims to play them with the intonation on the flat side. The e and the f , on the other hand, require a great deal more air if they are to sound 'free'.

✏ When using a tuning device to check, one finds that especially in the third register in pianissimo one is usually playing far too sharp. Our "clarinettist's ear" has unfortunately become all too accustomed to this sharpness in intonation, and it is therefore essential to check when practising! Good intonation is a real art in this register!

✏ In forte, on the other hand, the third register can also veer onto the flat side. The cause of this lies almost invariably in the reed being too soft.

✏ And to return once more to tone: free and supple in piano, full and warm in forte – this is no easy matter in the third register. **Plenty of practice and good reeds are a must here!**

✏ Extend this exercise too:

TIPPS:

✏ Die Töne im dritten Register haben völlig unterschiedliche Eigenschaften. Das des''', es''' , ges''' und das g''' gehen erstaunlich leicht, wenn man sie frei schwingen lässt und dunkel färbt. Sie brauchen viel weniger Luftdruck, als z. B. g'' oder c'''. Am besten gelingen sie, wenn man versucht, sie von der Intonation her tief zu spielen. Das e''' und das f''' brauchen dagegen sehr viel mehr Luft, um frei zu klingen.

✏ Bei der Kontrolle mit einem Stimmgerät wird man feststellen, dass man vor allem im Pianissimo im dritten Register meist viel zu hoch ist. Unser „klarinettistisches" Ohr hat sich an diese zu hohe Intonation leider sehr gewöhnt. Man übe also unbedingt kontrolliert! In dieser Lage ist gute Intonation eine Kunst!

✏ Im Forte dagegen kann das dritte Register auch zu tief werden. Dies liegt dann fast immer an einem zu leichten Blatt.

✏ Und noch einmal zum Klang: Im Piano frei und weich, im Forte voll und warm, das lässt sich im dritten Register nicht mehr so leicht machen. **Viel Übung und gute Blätter sind hier unerlässlich!**

✏ auch diese Übung erweitern:

28. ARTICULATION EXERCISE

AIM: The same aims and tips apply here as to all previous articulation exercises, especially no. 23.

EXECUTION: Play this exercise as in no. 5 but this time at the tempo ♩ = 120:

28. ARTIKULATIONSÜBUNG

ZIEL: Es gelten die gleichen Ziele und Tipps wie bei allen vorangegangenen Artikulationsübungen, vor allem bei Nr. 23.

AUSFÜHRUNG: Dieselbe Übung wie bei Nr. 5, nur diesmal im Tempo ♩ = 120 spielen:

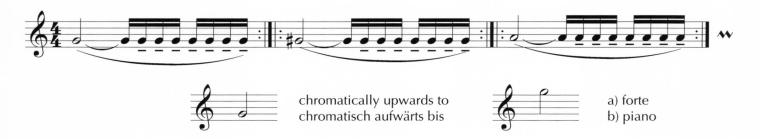

chromatically upwards to
chromatisch aufwärts bis

a) forte
b) piano

29. DYNAMICS EXERCISE

AIM: The same aims and tips apply here as to the exercises no.10 and no. 24.

EXECUTION: Play the same exercises as in no. 24 on the following notes (♩ = 60):

29. DYNAMIKÜBUNG

ZIEL: Es gelten die gleichen Ziele und Tipps wie bei den Übungen Nr. 10 und Nr. 24.

AUSFÜHRUNG: Dieselben Übungen wie bei Nr. 24 auf folgenden Tönen spielen (♩ = 60):

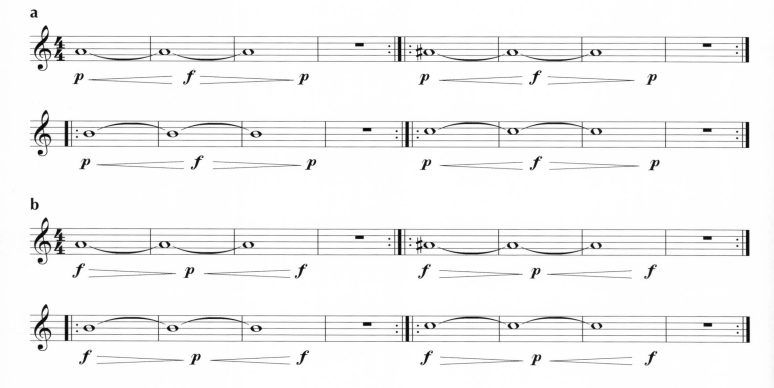

30. RESPONSE EXERCISE

AIM: The same aims and tips apply here as to all previous response exercises, especially no. 8.

EXECUTION: Play this exercise in the following rhythm and at tempo ♩ = 60:

30. ANBLASÜBUNG

ZIEL: Es gelten die gleichen Ziele und Tipps wie bei allen vorangegangenen Anblasübungen vor allem der Übung Nr. 8.

AUSFÜHRUNG: Im folgenden Rhythmus und im Tempo ♩ = 60 spielen:

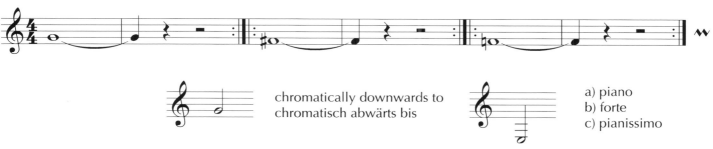

chromatically downwards to
chromatisch abwärts bis

a) piano
b) forte
c) pianissimo

TIPS:

- ✍ The final stage of the response exercises. The feeling for the varying tone and response of the different notes should now be fully developed, as well as a relaxed sequence of breathing in, "moment of repose" (with build-up of breath pressure) and note attack, with the throat region free and open and the minimum of movement at the front of the tongue.

- ✍ Here, too, it is most important that the difference in inner tension of the note as compared to that of the rest is kept to a minimum. **A rest is not without its inner tension!**

TIPPS:

- ✍ Die letzte Stufe der Anblasübungen. Jetzt sollte das Gefühl für den unterschiedlichen Klang und die unterschiedliche Ansprache der Töne voll entwickelt sein, ebenso wie ein lockerer Ablauf von Einatmung, Verhaltepause (mit Aufbau des Blasdrucks) und Anblasen des Tones mit freiem Rachenraum und minimaler Bewegung der vorderen Zunge.

- ✍ Wichtig ist auch hier, dass man den Spannungsunterschied zwischen Ton und Pause sehr klein hält. **Eine Pause ist nicht ohne Spannung!**

31. ARTICULATION EXERCISE

AIM: The same aims and tips apply here as to all previous articulation exercises, in particular no. 22 and no. 23.

EXECUTION: This is the same exercise as in no. 22 but this time play it at tempo ♩ = 120:

31. ARTIKULATIONSÜBUNG

ZIEL: Es gelten die gleichen Ziele und Tipps wie für alle vorangegangenen Artikulationsübungen vor allem Nr. 22 und Nr. 23.

AUSFÜHRUNG: Dieselbe Übung wie bei Nr. 22, nur diesmal im Tempo ♩ = 120 spielen:

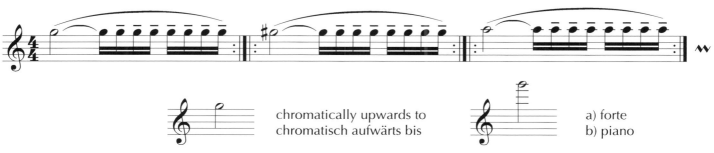

chromatically upwards to
chromatisch aufwärts bis

a) forte
b) piano

TIP:

- ✍ in this register and at this speed, skilful tonguing is what counts above all else; the slighter and lighter the movement of the tongue, the better.

TIPP:

- ✍ In dieser Lage und Geschwindigkeit kommt es vor allem auf die Geschicklichkeit der Zunge an, je kleiner und leichter die Zungenbewegung, desto besser.

32. DYNAMICS EXERCISE

AIM: The same aims and tips apply here as to the exercises no. 10 and no. 24.

EXECUTION: Play the following exercises at tempo ♩ = 60:

32. DYNAMIKÜBUNG

ZIEL: Es gelten die gleichen Ziele und Tipps wie bei den Übungen Nr. 10 und Nr. 24.

AUSFÜHRUNG: Folgende Übungen im Tempo ♩ = 60 spielen:

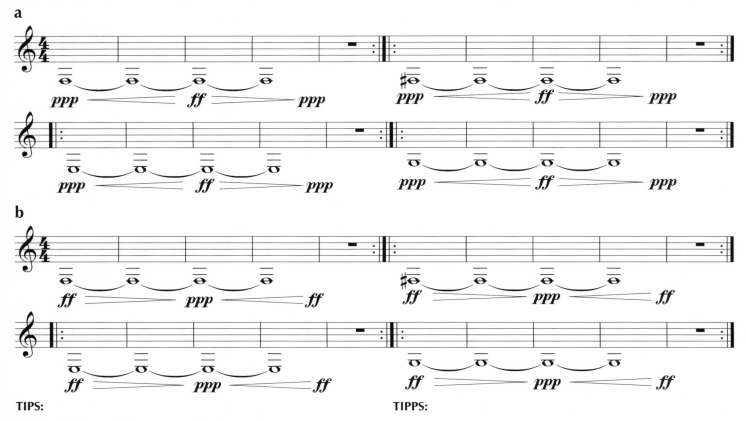

TIPS:

- In this exercise, the soft dynamics should be taken right down to the lowest limit.

- Take care not to prolong the decrescendo part of the exercise beyond that indicated (both in **a** and **b**).

- Here, once again, special attention should be given to evenness. In exercise **b**, it is also important not to remain dynamically static at the quietest point.

TIPPS:

- Die Dynamik im leisen Bereich soll jetzt bis an die untere Grenze gehen.

- Man achte darauf, dass der Decrescendo-Teil nicht länger wird, als er soll (sowohl bei **a** als auch bei **b**).

- Besondere Beachtung benötigt auch hier wieder die Gleichmäßigkeit. Man vermeide dabei auch, bei Übung **b** am leisesten Punkt eine Weile dynamisch zu verharren.

33. RESPONSE EXERCISE

AIM: The same aims and tips apply here as to all previous response exercises, in particular no. 4 and no. 30.

EXECUTION: Play the following notes in the same manner and rhythm as in exercise no. 30 (♩ = 60):

33. ANBLASÜBUNG

ZIEL: Es gelten die gleichen Ziele und Tipps wie bei allen Anblasübungen , vor allem bei Nr. 4 und Nr. 30.

AUSFÜHRUNG: In der Art und im Rhythmus wie bei der Übung Nr. 30 folgende Töne spielen (♩ = 60):

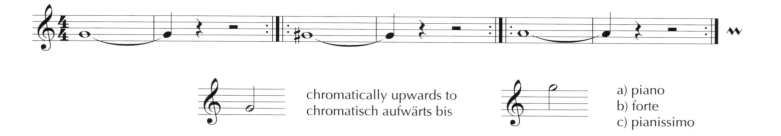

chromatically upwards to chromatisch aufwärts bis	a) piano b) forte c) pianissimo

34. ARTICULATION EXERCISE

AIM: The same aims and tips apply here as to all previous articulation exercises, in particular no. 23.

EXECUTION: This is the same exercise as no. 2 but play it this time at tempo ♩ = 138:

34. ARTIKULATIONSÜBUNG

ZIEL: Es gelten die gleichen Ziele und Tipps wie bei allen Artikulationsübungen, vor allem bei Nr. 23.

AUSFÜHRUNG: Dieselbe Übung wie bei Nr. 2, nur diesmal im Tempo ♩ = 138.

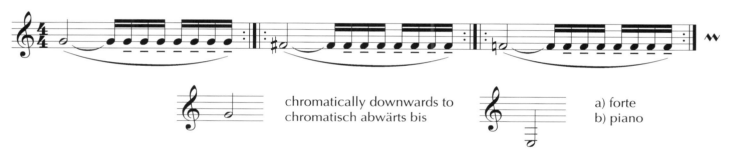

chromatically downwards to chromatisch abwärts bis	a) forte b) piano

TIPS:

✏ This will strike some players as being a "breakneck" tempo. This is usually due to the fact that the articulation sets in too late and is too ponderous. If one succeeds in playing (almost!) too early and avoiding starting problems, the tempo will suddenly become comfortably playable (for all!).

✏ Any player still having trouble can work up to this tempo by approaching it via ♩ = 126 and ♩ =132.

✏ The maximum tonguing speed varies greatly from individual to individual. Some clarinettists are capable of very fast single tonguing, but this appears to be inborn and thus not within everyone's reach, even with endless practice. But every player can attain his or her own "individual top speed". To achieve this, however, no complexes may be allowed to develop and one must practise intelligently! With intelligent practice any player can achieve a tonguing speed that is fast enough. **Relaxation makes for perfection!**

✏ Of course, those who find tempo ♩ =138 comfortable can opt for an even faster speed, but must take care that the tongue does not become fatigued.

TIPPS:

✏ Dieses Tempo wird manchem rasend schnell vorkommen. Meist liegt dies aber nur daran, dass die Artikulation zu spät und zu schwerfällig startet. Wenn man es schafft, (fast!) zu früh zu spielen und die Anlaufschwierigkeiten zu vermeiden, wird das Tempo plötzlich (und für jeden!) bequem spielbar.

✏ Wer trotzdem noch Schwierigkeiten hat, kann sich auch über die Tempi ♩ = 126 und ♩ = 132 an das Tempo heranarbeiten.

✏ Die maximale Geschwindigkeit der Artikulation ist individuell sehr verschieden. Es gibt Klarinettisten mit sehr schneller einfacher Zunge. Dies scheint angeboren zu sein und ist damit nicht von jedem erreichbar, auch nicht mit noch so viel Übung. Es kann aber jeder seine „individuelle Höchstgeschwindigkeit" erreichen. Dafür dürfen allerdings keine Komplexe auftreten und man muss klug üben! Eine ausreichend schnelle Artikulationsgeschwindigkeit kann bei klugem Üben von Jedem erlangt werden. **Lockerheit macht den Meister!**

✏ Natürlich können diejenigen, denen das Tempo ♩ =138 bequem vorkommt, das Tempo auch noch steigern, man achte nur darauf, dass die Zunge nicht ermüdet.

35. DYNAMICS EXERCISE

AIM: The same aims and tips apply here as to exercises no. 17 and no. 32.

EXECUTION: Play the following notes in the same manner and tempo (♩ = 60) as in exercise no. 32:

35. DYNAMIKÜBUNG

ZIEL: Es gelten die gleichen Ziele und Tipps wie bei den Übungen Nr. 17 und Nr. 32.

AUSFÜHRUNG: In derselben Art und im selben Tempo (♩ = 60) wie bei der Übung Nr. 32 die folgenden Töne spielen:

a

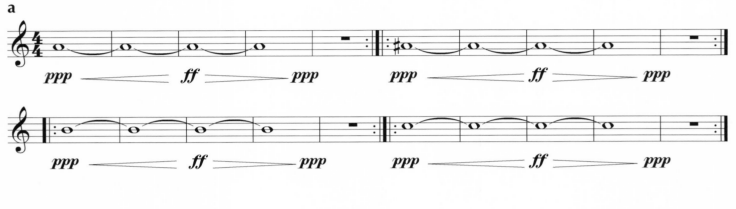

b

36. RESPONSE EXERCISE

AIM: The same aims and tips apply here as to exercises no. 15 and no. 30.

EXECUTION: Play the following notes in the same manner and rhythm as in exercise no. 30 (♩ = 60):

36. ANBLASÜBUNG

ZIEL: Es gelten die gleichen Ziele und Tipps wie für die Übungen Nr. 15 und Nr. 30.

AUSFÜHRUNG: In derselben Art und im selben Rhythmus wie bei der Übung Nr. 30 die folgenden Töne spielen (♩ = 60):

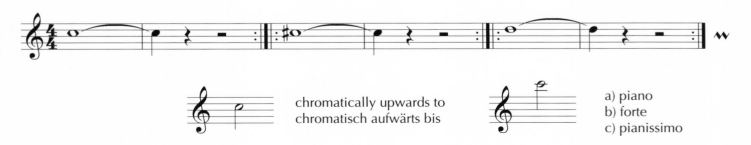

chromatically upwards to
chromatisch aufwärts bis

a) piano
b) forte
c) pianissimo

37. ARTICULATION EXERCISE

AIM: The same aims and tips apply here as to all previous articulation exercises, in particular no. 34.

EXECUTION: Play this exercise as no. 5 but this time at tempo ♩ = 138:

37. ARTIKULATIONSÜBUNG

ZIEL: Es gelten die gleichen Ziele und Tipps wie bei allen Artikulationsübungen, vor allem bei Nr. 34.

AUSFÜHRUNG: Dieselbe Übung wie bei Nr. 5, nur diesmal im Tempo ♩ = 138:

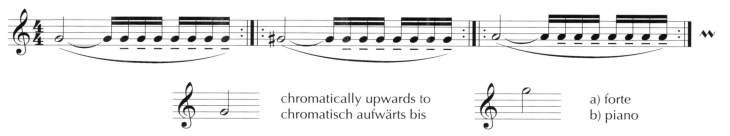

chromatically upwards to
chromatisch aufwärts bis

a) forte
b) piano

38. DYNAMICS EXERCISE

AIM: The aim of this exercise is the absolute command of breath control, the interplay of the embouchure (lip pressure, point of embouchure) and the throat (openness despite decrescendo) and breathing support.

EXECUTION: Play the following exercises

38. DYNAMIKÜBUNG

ZIEL: Ziel der Übung ist die absolute Kontrolle der Luftführung und des Zusammenwirkens von Ansatz (Lippendruck, Ansatzpunkt), Halsraum (Offenheit trotz Decrescendo) und Atemstütze.

AUSFÜHRUNG: Folgende Übungen

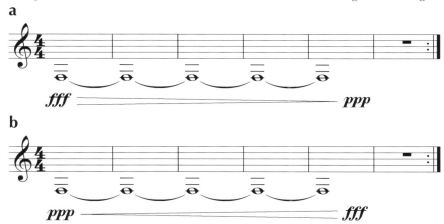

in tempo ♩ = 60 on the following notes:

im Tempo ♩ = 60 auf folgenden Tönen spielen:

re. **a**: The decrescendo should be spread perfectly evenly through the course of the entire long note, i.e. not as a rapid decrease of volume at the beginning of the note and a long pianissimo at the end. The critical point (given a normal reed) lies approximately in the middle of the dynamic range. On no account should the sound become duller from piano onwards; it should remain, as in forte, round, voluminous and with good carrying power throughout the note's duration. Above all, "pinching closed" the tone (by lips and jaw) is to be avoided. Even in pianissimo the reed must vibrate freely and along its entire length.

zu **a**: Das Decrescendo soll über den gesamten, sehr langen Ton hinweg absolut gleichmäßig sein, d. h. nicht am Anfang zu schnell zurückgehen und am Ende lange im Pianissimo verweilen. Der kritische Punkt liegt (ein normales Blatt vorausgesetzt) etwa in der Mitte des Dynamikbereichs. Der Klang sollte auf keinen Fall vom Piano an flacher werden, sondern über den ganzen Verlauf rund, voluminös und tragfähig sein wie im Forte. Dabei ist vor allem das „Abquetschen" des Klanges (durch Lippen und Kiefer) zu vermeiden. Das Blatt muss auch im Pianissimo frei und in voller Länge schwingen.

re. **b**: The tone should come from nowhere, but nevertheless the moment when this happens must be determined by the player. So it is a prerequisite to have already mastered the response exercises! The crescendo should again be very even, i. e. not slow at the start and quick at the end. The entire crescendo, free of pressure, must be generated by intensifying the air flow and increasing the air volume. The tone must become very loud without becoming shrill. Reeds that have no substance in fortissimo may make it comfortable to play the pianissimo but all in all they are unacceptable! The note should be rounded and controlled as it terminates and should not break off abruptly.

zu **b**: Der Ton soll aus dem Nichts kommen, trotzdem aber zu einem von uns kontrollierten Zeitpunkt. Die Beherrschung der Anblasübungen ist also Voraussetzung! Das Crescendo wiederum soll sehr gleichmäßig sein, d. h. nicht am Anfang langsam und am Ende schnell. Das gesamte Crescendo muss ohne Druck frei und offen durch die Intensivierung der Luftführung und durch die Steigerung der Luftmenge erzeugt werden. Der Ton soll sehr laut werden, ohne dabei zu schreien. Blätter, die im Fortissimo keine Substanz haben, sind vielleicht für das Pianissimo bequem, aber insgesamt unakzeptabel! Der Ton soll am Schluss rund und kontrolliert enden und nicht abgerissen werden.

TIPS:

✏ The most important criterion of the exercise is evenness; any fluctuation in tone, however slight, is a basic flaw.

✏ In view of the exercise length, it is obviously necessary to be very economical with the breath, i.e. blow very cleanly. The expending of any air other than to generate tone, i.e. any hissing, whether in pianissimo or in forte, must be avoided.

✏ It goes without saying that this exercise cannot be played using simply any reed. But one should still avoid blaming too much on the reed: With regular training, even mediocre reeds can be played cleanly!

TIPPS:

✏ Die Gleichmäßigkeit ist das wichtigste Kriterium der Übung, jede noch so kleine Tonschwankung ist grundsätzlich falsch.

✏ Man muss bei der Länge der Übung natürlich auch sehr ökonomisch blasen, d. h. sehr sauber. Jede Luft, welche nicht Ton wird, d. h. jedes Rauschen, ob im Pianissimo oder im Forte, muss vermieden werden.

✏ Diese Übung ist selbstverständlich nicht auf jedem Blatt realisierbar. Man vermeide jedoch, zu vieles auf das Blatt zu schieben: Bei regelmäßigem Training sind auch mittelmäßige Blätter sauber beherrschbar!

39. RESPONSE EXERCISE

AIM: The same aims and tips apply here as to all previous response exercises, in particular no. 21, no. 26 and no. 30.

EXECUTION: Play the following notes in the same manner and rhythm as in exercise no. 30 (♩ = 60):

39. ANBLASÜBUNG

ZIEL: Es gelten die gleichen Ziele und Tipps wie bei allen vorangegangenen Anblasübungen, vor allem Nr. 21, Nr. 26 und Nr. 30.

AUSFÜHRUNG: In derselben Art und im selben Rhythmus wie bei der Übung Nr. 30 die folgenden Töne spielen (♩ = 60):

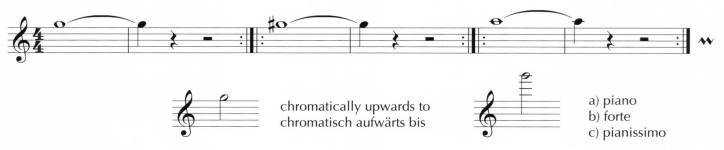

chromatically upwards to
chromatisch aufwärts bis

a) piano
b) forte
c) pianissimo

TIP:

✏ In addition to the problems of attack, it is not easy to keep the notes even in pianissimo. **This requires a great deal of practice!**

TIPP:

✏ Zusätzlich zu den Schwierigkeiten des Anblasens ist es im Pianissimo nicht einfach, die Töne gleichmäßig zu halten. **Dies braucht viel Übung!**

40. ARTICULATION EXERCISE

AIM: The same aims and tips apply here as to all previous articulation exercises, in particular no. 34 and no. 37.

EXECUTION: This is the same exercise as no. 31 but this time play it at tempo ♩ = 138:

40. ARTIKULATIONSÜBUNG

ZIEL: Es gelten die gleichen Ziele und Tipps wie bei allen vorangegangenen Artikulationsübungen vor allem bei Nr. 34 und Nr. 37.

AUSFÜHRUNG: Dieselbe Übung wie bei Nr. 31, nur diesmal im Tempo ♩ = 138 spielen:

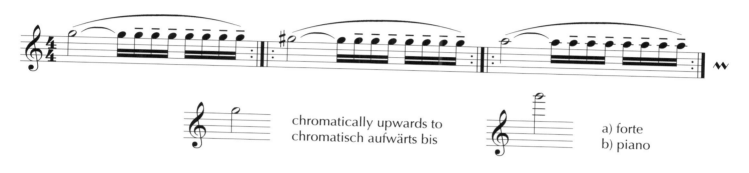

chromatically upwards to
chromatisch aufwärts bis

a) forte
b) piano

41. DYNAMICS EXERCISE

AIM: The same aims and tips apply here as to the previous dynamics exercises, especially no. 32 and no. 38.

EXECUTION: Play the following exercises at tempo ♩ = 60:

41. DYNAMIKÜBUNG

ZIEL: Es gelten die gleichen Ziele und Tipps wie bei den vorangegangenen Dynamikübungen, vor allem bei Nr. 32 und Nr. 38.

AUSFÜHRUNG: Folgende Übungen im Tempo ♩ = 60 spielen:

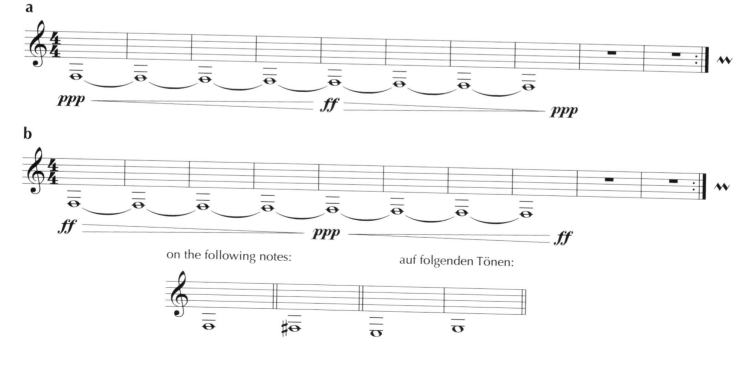

on the following notes:

auf folgenden Tönen:

42. ARTICULATION EXERCISE

AIM: The aim of this exercise is to achieve a light, short and springy staccato without interrupting the air flow or the breath control.

EXECUTION: Play this exercise at tempo ♩ = 120 employing the familiar rhythm:

42. ARTIKULATIONSÜBUNG

ZIEL: Ziel der Übung ist das Erreichen eines lockeren, kurzen und federnden Staccato ohne Unterbrechung des Luftstroms und der Luftführung.

AUSFÜHRUNG: Im Tempo ♩ = 120 und im bekannten Rhythmus:

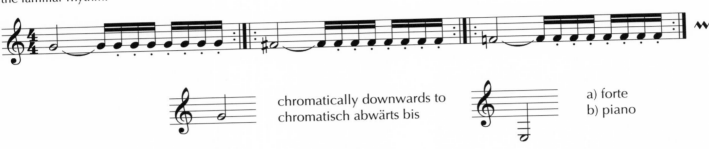

chromatically downwards to
chromatisch abwärts bis

a) forte
b) piano

but this time staccato, using the syllable "ta" instead of the soft syllable "da".

TIPS:

- It is essential that all the comments accompanying exercise no. 2 are read through once again. In principle, no basic changes are to be made for playing staccato as compared with portato, the only difference being that rather than being soft, the muscle at the tip of the tongue is now somewhat tauter.

- In spite of the shorter articulation, one should on no account have the impression of playing individual notes. Even in staccato, the result must be a line of notes; the stream of air must not be interrupted by the tongue movement which, by means of its elasticity, must be adjusted to suit the reed tension.

- The reed's vibration and the tongue's movement must support each other mutually. The tongue bounces off the reed just as the violinist's bow bounces off the string in spiccato. To achieve this, a reed is required which has the necessary tension, of course! Furthermore, this staccato is only possible from a certain tempo upwards. A slow, springy staccato is very hard to accomplish!

- Should this exercise present problems at first, it is helpful to begin by playing the first tongued notes as usual in portato and then shift into staccato during articulation. This should not become a habit, however, but simply offer assistance for getting started.

spielen, doch diesmal nicht mit der weichen Silbe „da" sondern mit der Silbe „ta", also im Staccato.

TIPPS:

- Es ist unbedingt noch einmal alles bei Übung Nr. 2 Gesagte durchzulesen. Im Prinzip soll sich gegenüber dem Portato im Staccato nichts ändern. Der einzige Unterschied ist, dass der Zungenmuskel an der Spitze nicht so weich ist, sondern mehr angespannt.

- Auch die kürzere Artikulation darf keinesfalls dazu führen, dass man das Gefühl hat, einzelne Töne zu spielen. Es muss auch im Staccato eine Linie von Tönen werden, die Zungenbewegung darf den Luftstrom nicht unterbrechen, sie muss sich der Spannung des Blattes federnd anpassen.

- Die Schwingung des Blattes und die Bewegung der Zunge müssen sich gegenseitig unterstützen. Die Zunge federt vom Blatt ab wie der Bogen des Geigers beim Spiccato von der Saite federt. Dazu ist natürlich ein Blatt notwendig, welches auch über Spannung verfügt! Außerdem ist dieses Staccato erst ab einer gewissen Geschwindigkeit möglich. Ein langsames, federndes Staccato ist sehr schwierig!

- Sollte die Übung am Beginn Schwierigkeiten bereiten, empfiehlt es sich, zunächst die ersten artikulierten Noten wie gewohnt im Portato zu beginnen und beim Artikulieren ins Staccato überzugehen. Dies sollte aber nicht zur Gewohnheit werden, sondern eine Hilfe für den Anfang bleiben.

43. ARTICULATION EXERCISE

AIM: The same aims and tips apply here as to exercise no. 42.

EXECUTION: Play the following notes in the same manner as in exercise no. 42 (staccato) and at tempo ♩ = 120:

43. ARTIKULATIONSÜBUNG

ZIEL: Es gelten die gleichen Ziele und Tipps wie bei Übung Nr. 42.

AUSFÜHRUNG: In derselben Art wie bei der Übung Nr. 42 (Staccato) und im Tempo ♩ = 120 die folgenden Töne spielen:

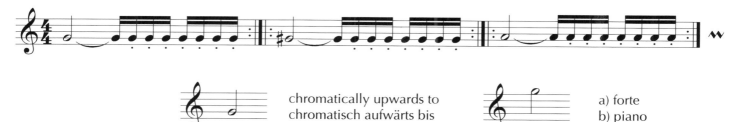

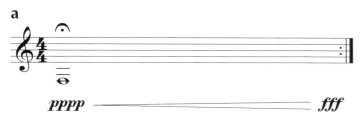

chromatically upwards to
chromatisch aufwärts bis

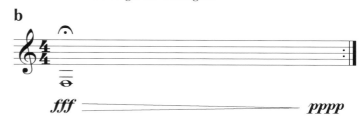

a) forte
b) piano

44. DYNAMICS EXERCISE

AIM: A final dynamics exercise aimed at achieving the greatest possible stability, control and stamina in breath control.

EXECUTION: Play the following exercises:

44. DYNAMIKÜBUNG

ZIEL: Eine letzte Dynamikübung. Ziel der Übung ist größtmögliche Stabilität, Kontrolle und Kondition bei der Atemführung.

AUSFÜHRUNG: Folgende Übungen:

a

$pppp$ ——————————— fff

on the following notes:

b

fff ——————————— $pppp$

auf folgenden Tönen spielen:

The notes should be held as long as possible – this is a matter of air volume, breath control, breath allocation, self-estimation and also relaxation! **The psyche plays a not inconsiderable role here!**

Die Töne sollen so lang wie möglich gehalten werden. Eine Frage des Atemvolumens, der Atemkontrolle, der Atemeinteilung, der Selbsteinschätzung und auch der Lockerheit! **Die Psyche spielt dabei keine geringe Rolle!**

TIPS:

- Obviously the breath has to be well allocated, especially since the crescendo (or decrescendo) should be very evenly spread (the mezzoforte constitutes the real midpoint of the long note). Care must be taken – above all in forte – that no more air is expended than is really necessary for producing the tone.

- It is also essential to ensure that firstly, the shoulders are not raised and secondly, in the decrescendo the note does not tremble as it nears its end.

- Incidentally, it is – strangely enough – possible to continue playing this exercise longer on harder reeds than on softer ones!

TIPPS:

- Selbstverständlich muss man sich den Atem gut einteilen, vor allem, da das Crescendo (bzw. Decrescendo) sehr gleichmäßig sein soll (das Mezzoforte bildet also wirklich die Mitte des langen Tons). Vor allem im Forte-Bereich muss man daher aufpassen, dass man nicht mehr Luft abgibt, als für die Tonerzeugung wirklich nötig ist.

- Weiter ist unbedingt darauf zu achten, dass erstens nicht die Schultern hochgezogen werden und dass zweitens nicht im Decrescendo gegen Ende der Ton zittert.

- Übrigens kann man diese Übung merkwürdigerweise auf schwereren Blättern eher länger spielen, als auf leichteren!

45. ARTICULATION EXERCISE

AIM: The same aims and tips apply here as to exercises no. 42 and no.43.

EXECUTION: Play the following notes as in exercise no. 42 (staccato) at tempo ♩ = 120:

45. ARTIKULATIONSÜBUNG

ZIEL: Es gelten die gleichen Ziele und Tipps wie bei den Übungen Nr. 42 und Nr. 43.

AUSFÜHRUNG: In derselben Art wie bei Übung Nr. 42 (Staccato) und im Tempo ♩ = 120 folgende Töne spielen:

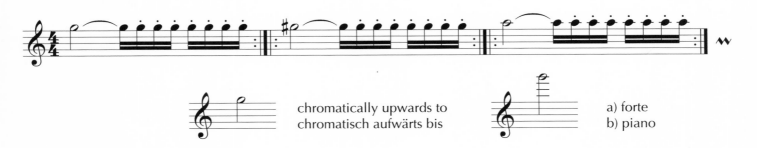

chromatically upwards to
chromatisch aufwärts bis

a) forte
b) piano

FINAL REMARKS:

Having mastered all 45 exercises securely and with a good tone, the player should be in a position to cope with even the most difficult demands of the solo clarinet repertoire and the orchestral literature as far as tone is concerned. However, beware of thinking that one only needs to work through this sound exercise programme once in a lifetime! Inevitably, parts of these fundamental exercises, at the least, belong to the daily practice schedule of any good clarinettist!

Anyone who would like to take the exercises further can practise the staccato exercises no. 42, no. 43 and no. 45 at slower and faster tempi. With slower tempi, where the emphasis is more on the sound aspect, the exercises are not easy. With faster tempi, care must be taken above all to avoid any complexes developing! If consistent attention is paid to tone and relaxation, each and every player can acquire a staccato that is fast enough!

SCHLUSSBEMERKUNG:

Wer nun alle 45 Übungen sicher und tonschön beherrscht, sollte im klanglichen Bereich in der Lage sein, auch die schwierigsten Anforderungen des solistischen Klarinetten-Repertoires und der Orchester-Literartur zu meistern. Man hüte sich allerdings sehr vor der Meinung, dass man das Programm dieser Klangübungen nur einmal in seinem Leben durchmachen müsse! Zumindest Teile aus diesen Basis-übungen gehören unausweichlich zum täglichen Übungs-pensum eines jeden guten Klarinettisten!

Wer die Übungen noch fortführen will, kann die Staccato-Übungen Nr. 42, Nr. 43 und Nr. 45 in langsameren und schnelleren Tempi üben. Langsamere Tempi gehen mehr in den klanglichen Bereich und sind nicht einfach. Bei schnelle-ren Tempi hüte man sich vor allem vor Komplexen! Wenn man konsequent auf den Klang und die Lockerheit achtet, ist wirklich jedem ein ausreichend schnelles Staccato möglich!

No other aspect of playing an instrument is as crucial to musical interpretation as the ability to articulate freely, cleanly, with differentiation and sometimes also at considerable speed. But in this area, especially in the case of wind instruments, there is apparently no justice in the way joys and woes are dealt out: What is natural and inborn to one player appears completely out of reach to another and, so it seems, is a clear sign of his or her own shortcomings. This is due – amongst other things – to the fact that up to now, scarcely any exercises have been available dealing in a genuinely analytical way with the articulation problems that can arise. To address this situation, the following exercises are intended to provide units that are thorough and, above all, basic at first, with slow and gradual progression to follow. Analysis of the articulation processes on a wind instrument is a relatively complex business, as most of these processes take place within the body and are hardly visible externally. Added to this is the fact that the very parts of the body involved in articulation (trunk and chest muscles, diaphragm, shoulder girdle, throat region, mouth muscles, and tongue) cannot be controlled entirely at will but are subject to all kinds of mental influences. Nevertheless, many years of experience have shown that every clarinettist can develop articulation sufficient to do justice to his or her artistic ambitions, as long as the processes of movement involved in articulation are well understood and a practice programme adhered to which covers the various sub-aspects of articulation as systematic units. The exercises that follow here offer such a programme.

It makes sense to begin by describing the different sub-aspects of articulation on the clarinet:
The first – and without doubt the most important – criterion is the tone quality of the articulated notes. This aspect has been dealt with at length in the sound exercises nos. 2, 5, 9 and 13, and initially it is advisable to wait before embarking on the following exercises until the sound exercises referred to pose no more problems; secondly, the text accompanying those exercises should be reread for a reminder of what our goal is here: an optimal process of tongue movement, i.e. as slight as possible, which has to be controlled and checked on the basis of optimal tone!

The second aspect can be demonstrated by means of an example: there are many clarinettists who have no trouble playing the exercises cited but who, when it comes to playing individual notes or just a few notes in staccato, scarcely manage to produce a single one that is genuinely controlled. These players will never be in a position to play the opening of the third movement of Mozart's Clarinet Concerto with the degree of sophistication they would wish. In such cases, which are by no means uncommon, there is a lack of basic flexibility of the tongue and, hence, of tonguing speed for individual note attack. Only with thorough practice will it become possible for us to manage these key moments without needing to "cheat".

Wohl kein Aspekt des Instrumentalspiels hat für die Interpretation von Musik so wesentliche Bedeutung wie die Fähigkeit zu lockerer, sauberer, differenzierter und bisweilen auch sehr schneller Artikulation. Leider liegen auf diesem Gebiet vor allem bei den Blasinstrumenten Freud und Leid scheinbar höchst ungerecht verteilt: Was dem Einen wie selbstverständlich und angeboren vorkommt, erscheint dem Anderen völlig unerreichbar und als offenkundiges Beispiel eigenen Unvermögens. Dies liegt sicher auch daran, dass es bisher kaum Übungen gibt, die sich den Problemen, welche bei der Artikulation auftreten können, wirklich analytisch nähern. In den nachfolgenden Übungen soll versucht werden, durch gründliche und vor allem einfach beginnende und langsam fortschreitende Einheiten diesem Missstand entgegenzuwirken. Zwar sind die Vorgänge der Artikulation auf einem Blasinstrument relativ kompliziert zu analysieren, weil die meisten Bewegungen sich im Inneren des Körpers abspielen und nach außen kaum sichtbar werden. Zudem sind gerade die an der Artikulation beteiligten Körperregionen (Rumpf- und Brustmuskulatur, Zwerchfell, Schultergürtel, Halsbereich, Mundmuskulatur, Zunge) nicht nur willentlich zu steuern, sondern vielfältigen psychischen Einflüssen ausgesetzt. Trotz allem zeigt langjährige Erfahrung, dass jeder Klarinettist seine Artikulation so weit bringen kann, dass sie künstlerischen Ansprüchen gerecht wird, wenn die Bewegungsabläufe der Artikulation verstanden werden und mit Geduld ein Übeprogramm eingehalten wird, welches alle durchaus verschiedenen Teilaspekte der Artikulation in systematischen Einheiten behandelt. Solch ein Programm soll mit den nachfolgenden Übungen angeboten werden.

Zunächst ist es sinnvoll, sich die verschiedenen Teilbereiche der Artikulation auf einer Klarinette vor Augen zu führen:
Das erste – und mit Sicherheit wichtigste – Kriterium ist die Klangqualität der artikulierten Noten. Dieser Aspekt wurde ganz ausführlich in den Klangstudien Nr. 2, 5, 9 und 13 behandelt, und es empfiehlt sich erstens, die folgenden Übungen nicht zu beginnen, bevor die genannten Klangübungen keine Schwierigkeiten mehr machen, und zweitens, noch einmal dort nachzulesen, um was es geht: Einen optimalen, d. h. geringstmöglichen Bewegungsablauf der Zunge, den man am optimalen Klang kontrollieren muss!

Der zweite Aspekt sei an einem Beispiel demonstriert: Es gibt viele Klarinettisten, welche die genannten Klangübungen mühelos beherrschen, aber bei einzelnen oder wenigen Staccato-Tönen kaum einen wirklich kontrollierten Ton hervorbringen. Den Anfang des 3. Satzes des Klarinettenkonzertes von Mozart werden diese Klarinettisten nie so differenziert spielen können, wie sie es sich vorstellen würden. In diesem nicht seltenen Fall mangelt es der Zunge an grundlegender Lockerheit und damit Geschwindigkeit im einzelnen Anstoß. Nur gründliche Übung wird uns in die Lage versetzen, in den entscheidenden Momenten nicht „mogeln" zu müssen.

A further section of the exercises concerns the ability to differentiate. The main consideration here is that articulated notes have to be structured. This is necessary because all music has to be phrased, i.e. organised, and on the other hand, good structuring in articulation can save extraordinary amounts of energy. In this context, a little practice can unleash potential previously undreamt of.

The fourth criterion is the one most readers have no doubt been waiting for impatiently, since for them it is the most important criterion, the crucial one – or perhaps even the only one: the speed of the tongue! But this one-sided fixation on speed constitutes a major part of the problem, and even if it sounds almost too good to be true, when the areas of tone, relaxation and structure have been mastered well, the speed problem usually solves itself! It is essential that one consideration is borne in mind, however: the possible top-speed for tongue movement is inborn, varies individually and, hence, cannot be increased beyond a certain point. If one manages to solve the technical issues by means of targeted exercises, it should also be possible to dispel the complexes that very often stand in the way of progress. Experience shows that almost any player can reach their "individual top-speed" which will be sufficient for the main areas of the musical spectrum. A sub-aspect of this matter is, however, the condition of the tongue muscle. As far as sheer "fitness" is concerned, intelligent and regular practice is – as in sport – a necessity.

The final point to be noted is, oddly enough, often vastly underestimated, despite being of prime importance: if the articulation involves not simply one and the same note, the main source of error is poor synchronisation between fingers and tongue. Usually this leads to near-total breakdown of all playing systems, the shock causing the throat region to narrow, the tongue to seize up and the fingers to stiffen. Rather than analysing the root causes of this, most players mistakenly assume that they are simply "unable to play staccato". This part of the topic is also to be approached slowly and thoroughly in the exercises, but the overriding principle is that all the note combinations to be articulated must already function perfectly in legato!

A final set of exercises will follow: suggestions for practising double tonguing. Double tonguing is regularly and frequently used by flutists, oboists, bassoonists and brass players. Nowadays there are also more and more clarinettists who have successfully mastered double tonguing. On the clarinet this is certainly rather more difficult than on the other wind instruments, mainly because a relatively large portion of the mouthpiece is in the player's mouth. Additional difficulties are 1) managing to achieve a similar tone with the articulating syllables "ta" and "ka" – on hard reeds, in particular, the "ka" does not speak as well – and 2) again, the problem with synchronisation of fingers and tongue. But these things can be practised, and the advantage resulting for all clarinettists who tackle the issue of double tonguing is not to be underestimated.

Ein weiterer Teil der Übungen betrifft die Fähigkeit zu differenzieren. Hier geht es vor allem darum, dass artikulierte Noten strukturiert werden müssen. Dies ist einmal erforderlich, weil jede Musik phrasiert, also gegliedert werden muss, andererseits kann eine gute Struktur in der Artikulation unglaublich viel Kraft sparen. Mit einiger Übung können hier ungeahnte Potenziale freiwerden.

Das vierte Kriterium ist jenes, auf welches sicher die meisten Leser bis jetzt schon ungeduldig gewartet haben, weil es für sie das wichtigste, das entscheidende – vielleicht sogar das einzige Kriterium darstellt: Die Geschwindigkeit der Zunge! Leider ist aber diese einseitige Fixierung auf die Geschwindigkeit ein großer Teil des Problems, und es klingt fast zu schön, um wahr zu sein: Wenn die Bereiche Klang, Lockerheit und Struktur gut beherrscht werden, ist das Problem Geschwindigkeit meist von alleine gelöst! Allerdings sollte man unbedingt eines dabei beachten: Die mögliche Höchstgeschwindigkeit der Zungenbewegung ist angeboren, individuell verschieden und damit von einem gewissen Punkt an nicht weiter steigerbar. Wenn man es schafft, mit gezielten Übungen die technischen Fragen zu lösen, sollten sich auch Komplexe aufheben lassen, die sehr häufig den Fortschritt behindern. Erfahrungsgemäß ist dann nahezu jedem eine „individuelle Höchstgeschwindigkeit" möglich, die den wesentlichen Bereichen der Musik genügen wird. Ein Teilaspekt auf diesem Gebiet ist dann allerdings die Kondition des Zungenmuskels. Für die reine Kondition ist – wie im Bereich des Sports – ein intelligentes und regelmäßiges Üben notwendig.

Der letzte Punkt, der zu beachten wäre, wird merkwürdigerweise trotz seiner eminenten Wichtigkeit meist völlig unterschätzt: Findet Artikulation nicht auf ein-und-demselben Ton statt, so ist die Hauptquelle für Fehler die mangelnde Synchronisation zwischen Fingern und Zunge. Meist gelingt dann fast gar nichts mehr, weil vor Schreck auch noch der Halsbereich verengt wird, die Zunge blockiert und die Finger verkrampfen. Anstatt die Ursachen zu analysieren, gewinnen die meisten dann irrigerweise die Erkenntnis, dass sie eben „kein Staccato könnten". Auch diesem Teilbereich soll sich in den Übungen langsam und gründlich genähert werden, wobei als oberstes Prinzip gelten muss, dass alle zu artikulierenden Tonverbindungen im Legato absolut optimal ablaufen müssen!

Eine letzte Übungsfolge wird sich dann anschließen: Vorschläge für Übungen der Doppelzunge. Die Doppelzunge wird von Flötisten, Oboisten, Fagottisten und Blechbläsern regelmäßig und häufig angewandt. In der letzten Zeit gibt es auch mehr und mehr Klarinettisten, welche die Doppelzunge beherrschen. Sicher sind die Gegebenheiten bei der Klarinette etwas schwieriger, als bei den anderen Blasinstrumenten, vor allem, weil man einen relativ großen Teil des Mundstücks im Mund hat. Weitere Schwierigkeiten sind der klangliche Angleich der Artikulationssilben „ta" und „ka" – besonders auf schwereren Blättern spricht das „ka" nicht so gut an – und

Finally, we turn to one factor that should on no account be neglected in this connection: the properties of the clarinet reed, in particular its strength and flexibility. Articulation becomes considerably more difficult from a certain strength onwards. Those players who, in their desire for a big, voluminous tone, choose very hard reeds will have to accept that in return they will lose out in terms of response when tonguing. On the other hand, this certainly does not mean that soft reeds always speak well: the decisive factor for the quality of a reed is not its strength but its elasticity. The reed must hold sufficient tension to spring back rapidly into its initial position. But this is not given in the case of many soft reeds, with the result that no easy articulation is possible here, either. So the solution must lie between the two extremes, and experience shows that these days, it is more common for players to choose reeds that are too soft than reeds that are too hard.

The ideal clarinet reed, therefore, has both elasticity and tension. In articulation, this elastic tension must not be impeded or lessened by the tongue, but rather exploited in support of the tongue-tip's movement. If we succeed in this, the whole process will function practically of its own accord!

wieder die Synchronisation von Fingern und Zunge. Aber diese Dinge lassen sich üben, und es ist sicher von nicht zu unterschätzendem Vorteil, wenn sich jeder Klarinettist auch mit der Doppelzunge beschäftigt.

Abschließend noch ein Faktor, den man bei diesem Thema auf keinen Fall vernachlässigen sollte: Die Beschaffenheit des Klarinettenblattes, vor allem seine Stärke und seine Flexibilität. Ab einer gewissen Stärke der Blätter wird die Artikulation sehr erschwert. Wer also für das Erreichen eines großen, voluminösen Tons auf sehr schwere Blätter setzt, muss dafür Einbußen in der Ansprache der Artikulation in Kauf nehmen. Andererseits bedeutet dies keinesfalls, dass leichte Blätter immer gut ansprechen: Entscheidend für die Qualität eines Blattes ist nicht die Stärke, sondern die Elastizität. Das Blatt muss über genügend Spannung verfügen, um schnell in die Ausgangslage zurückfedern zu können. Das wiederum ist bei vielen leichten Blättern nicht gegeben, und auch dann ist eine lockere Artikulation unmöglich. Die Lösung liegt also wohl in der Mitte, wobei die Erfahrung zeigt, dass heute eher zu leichte Blätter als zu schwere verwendet werden.

Das ideale Klarinettenblatt ist also mit einer federnden Spannung ausgestattet. Diese Spannung dürfen wir bei der Artikulation mit der Zunge nicht behindern oder dämpfen sondern müssen sie ganz im Gegenteil zur Unterstützung des Bewegungsablaufs der Zungenspitze nutzen. Wenn uns das gelingt, geht alles fast von selbst!

1. SOUND EXERCISE

AIM: The purpose of this exercise is to achieve evenness in tone between shorter and broader articulation.

EXECUTION: Play the following exercise in an easy dynamic (mp or mf) and at a quick but not strenuous tempo (♩ = 120 – 126):

1. KLANGÜBUNG

ZIEL: Die Übung bezweckt den klanglichen Ausgleich zwischen kürzerer und breiterer Artikulation.

AUSFÜHRUNG: Folgende Übung in einer entspannten Dynamik (mp oder mf) und in einem schnellen, aber nicht angestrengten Tempo (♩ = 120 – 126) spielen:

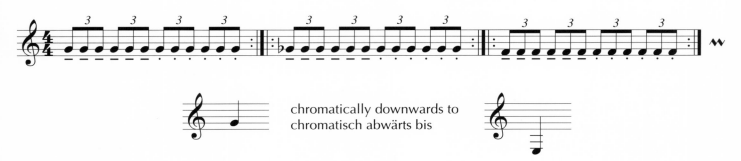

chromatically downwards to
chromatisch abwärts bis

TIPS:

✏ The shorter articulation must not be allowed to result in a narrower tone than the broader.

✏ Special attention must be given to the throat region. Here, as little as possible should change between the two types of articulation. The difference in articulation is brought about by the shaping and tension of the tongue muscle and the speed of the tongue, in addition to the length of time it remains on the reed.

✏ It is very revealing to try singing the exercise, meanwhile ensuring that the lower jaw stays relaxed and does not move together with the tongue during articulation.

ALTERNATIVES:

1.) Play the exercise in pianissimo and also in a robust forte.
2.) Play the exercise at a markedly slower tempo (♩ = 88 – 96).

TIPPS:

✏ Die kürzere Artikulation darf nicht enger klingen als die breitere.

✏ Man achte besonders auf den Halsbereich. Hier sollte sich zwischen den Artikulationsarten so wenig wie möglich ändern. Den Unterschied in der Artikulation bewirken Form und Spannung des Zungenmuskels sowie die Geschwindigkeit der Zunge und die Verweildauer am Blatt.

✏ Es ist sehr aufschlussreich, die Übung einmal zu singen, wobei beim Singen unbedingt darauf zu achten ist, dass der Unterkiefer locker ist und sich nicht bei der Artikulation mit der Zunge mitbewegt.

VARIANTEN:

1.) Die Übung im Pianissimo und auch im gesunden Forte spielen.
2.) Die Übungen in deutlich langsamerem Tempo spielen (♩ = 88 – 96).

2. SOUND EXERCISES

AIM: Again, these exercises are aimed at achieving a full, unhindered tone in the given articulation.

EXECUTION: Play the following exercises in an easy dynamic (mp or mf) and at a quick but not strenuous tempo (♩ = 116 – 120):

2. KLANGÜBUNGEN

ZIEL: Auch diese Übungen zielen darauf, in der Artikulation einen vollen, unbehinderten Klang zu erreichen.

AUSFÜHRUNG: Folgende Übungen in einer entspannten Dynamik (mp oder mf) und in einem schnellen, aber nicht angestrengten Tempo (♩ = 116 –120) spielen:

TIPS:

- ✎ All long notes should have as full and clean a tone as possible and finish resonantly.

- ✎ The transition from the longer notes to the staccato must be seamless, i.e. without a gap, which means that the larynx region remains open.

- ✎ The exercises **c** and **d** should be structured by means of a light stressing of the beginning of the bar and an easing of tension for the rest of the bar. In this way they should sound relaxed and not require too much energy to play.

ALTERNATIVES:

1.) Play the exercise in pianissimo and also in a robust forte.
2.) Play the exercise at a markedly slower tempo (♩ = 80 – 88).
3.) Play the exercises at a very rapid tempo. The exercises **c** and **d** then take a good deal of energy to play (no tensing up!). They are also good as training exercises for building up stamina.

TIPPS:

- ✎ Alle langen Noten sollen möglichst voll und sauber klingen und offen enden.

- ✎ Der Übergang von den längeren Noten zum Staccato muss nahtlos sein, d. h. ohne ein Loch. Der Kehlbereich bleibt also offen.

- ✎ Die Übungen **c** und **d** sollen durch leichtes Betonen der Taktanfänge und Entspannen des restlichen Taktes strukturiert werden. Sie sollen dadurch locker klingen und nicht zuviel Kraft benötigen.

VARIANTEN:

1.) Die Übungen im Pianissimo und auch im gesunden Forte spielen.
2.) Die Übungen in deutlich langsamerem Tempo spielen (♩ = 80 bis 88).
3.) Die Übungen in sehr schnellem Tempo spielen. Die Übungen **c** und **d** kosten dann doch viel Kraft (locker bleiben!). Sie eignen sich auch zum Training der Kondition.

3. SOUND EXERCISES

AIM: The same aim and tips apply here as to exercise no. 2.

EXECUTION: Play the following exercises in an easy dynamic (mp or mf) and at a quick but not strenuous tempo (♩ = 116 – 120):

3. KLANGÜBUNGEN

ZIEL: Für diese Übung gelten das gleiche Ziel und die gleichen Tipps wie für die Übung Nr. 2.

AUSFÜHRUNG: Folgende Übungen in einer entspannten Dynamik (mp oder mf) und in einem schnellen, aber nicht angestrengten Tempo (♩ = 116 – 120) spielen:

chromatically downwards to
chromatisch abwärts bis

TIPS:

✆ As for the previous exercises: light staccati, long notes with full sound, no gaps at transitions; phrase the exercises well so that they do not require much energy to play.

✆ In the case of exercises **c** and **d**, care must be taken that the stress does not slip on to the wrong notes, thereby placing the stress on the long notes. The emphasis should always be on the first note.

ALTERNATIVES:

1.) Play the exercise in pianissimo and also in a robust forte.
2.) Play the exercise at a markedly slower tempo (♩ = 80 – 88).
3.) Play the exercises at a very rapid tempo.

TIPPS:

✆ Wie bei den vorrangegangenen Übungen: Lockere Staccati, voll klingende lange Noten, keine Löcher bei den Übergängen, Übungen gut phrasieren, damit sie wenig Kraft kosten.

✆ Bei den Übungen **c** und **d** achte man darauf, dass nicht die Betonung „verrutscht", und die längeren Noten betont werden. Der Schwerpunkt soll immer auf der ersten Note liegen.

VARIANTEN:

1.) Die Übungen im Pianissimo und auch im gesunden Forte spielen.
2.) Die Übungen in deutlich langsameren Tempo spielen (♩ = 80 bis 88).
3.) Die Übungen in sehr schnellem Tempo spielen.

4. LOOSENING-UP EXERCISE

AIM: The aim of the loosening-up exercises is to optimise the tongue action and to train speed and freeness of the movements.

EXECUTION: Play the following exercises in an easy dynamic (mp or mf) and at a quick but not strenuous tempo (♩ = 112 – 120):

4. LOCKERUNGSÜBUNG

ZIEL: Ziel der Lockerungsübungen ist es, den Bewegungsverlauf der Zunge zu optimieren und Schnelligkeit und Lockerheit der Bewegungen zu trainieren.

AUSFÜHRUNG: Folgende Übungen in einer entspannten Dynamik (mp oder mf) und in einem schnellen, aber nicht angestrengten Tempo (♩ = 112 bis 120) spielen:

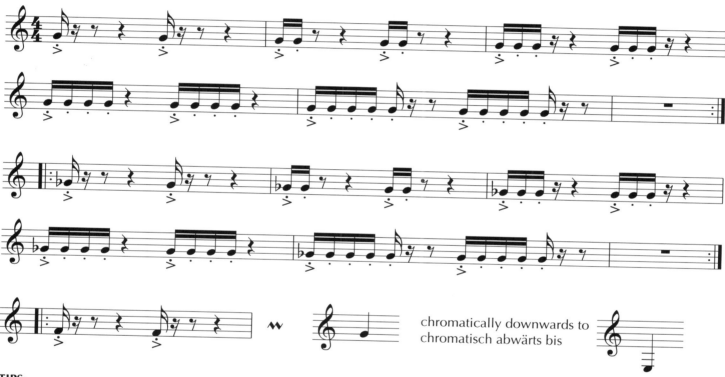

chromatically downwards to
chromatisch abwärts bis

TIPS:

☞ The syllable with which the staccato is produced is a not-too-hard "ta"; the larynx region is open. The tongue should be able to move freely and when performing the first attack (and also in the case of the single notes) it should, as a result of being relaxed, move very rapidly.

☞ The staccato notes should "bounce off" from the first note; no notes should seem to be separate entities, instead the impression should always be of lines of notes.

☞ The tone of the first notes is important right from the first bar on. It should be clean, free and full. Only if and when this is the case is the tongue movement sufficiently slight.

☞ If the first tone sounds dull and impure, too much of the back part of the tongue is moving in the throat cavity. In this case, one should revisit once more the articulation exercises nos. 2, 5, 9 and 13 in the chapter "Sound exercises".

TIPPS:

☞ Die Tonsilbe für das Staccato bildet ein nicht zu hartes „ta", der Kehlkopfbereich ist offen. Die Zunge soll frei beweglich sein und sich beim ersten Anstoß (auch beim einzelnen Anstoß) durch die Lockerheit sehr schnell bewegen.

☞ Die Staccato Töne sollen sich von der ersten Note abfedern, es sollen keine einzelnen Töne empfunden werden sondern Linien von Tönen.

☞ Wichtig ist vom ersten Takt an der Klang der ersten Noten. Er soll sauber, frei und voll sein. Nur wenn das der Fall ist, ist die Zungenbewegung klein genug.

☞ Wenn der erste Ton stumpf und unsauber klingt, bewegt sich noch zuviel vom hinteren Teil der Zunge im Rachenraum. In diesem Fall sollte man noch einmal auf die Artikulationsübungen Nr. 2, 5, 9 und 13 im Kapitel „Klangstudien" zurückgehen.

✏ It helps to observe the full bar's rest as this allows the tongue the opportunity to relax somewhat.

ALTERNATIVES:

1.) Play the exercises in pianissimo and also in a robust forte.
2.) Play the exercises at a markedly slower tempo (♩ = 80 – 88).

✏ Es ist hilfreich, den Pausentakt zu beachten, die Zunge kann dann wieder ein wenig entspannen.

VARIANTEN:

1.) Die Übungen im Pianissimo und auch im gesunden Forte spielen.
2.) Die Übungen in deutlich langsameren Tempo spielen (♩ = 80 bis 88).

5. LOOSENING-UP EXERCISE

AIM: The central goal of these exercises is, again, the velocity and looseness of the tongue movement.

EXECUTION: Play the following exercises in an easy dynamic (mp or mf) and at a quick but not strenuous tempo (♩ = 112 – 120):

5. LOCKERUNGSÜBUNG

ZIEL: Auch bei diesen Übungen geht es um die Schnelligkeit und Lockerheit der Zungenbewegung.

AUSFÜHRUNG: Folgende Übungen in einer entspannten Dynamik (mp oder mf) und in einem schnellen, aber nicht angestrengten Tempo (♩ = 112 bis 120) spielen:

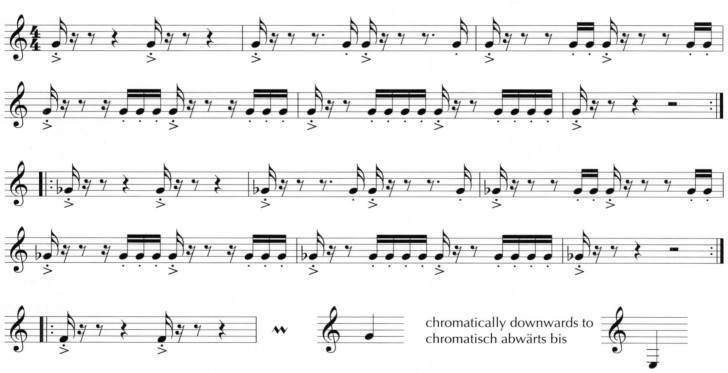

chromatically downwards to
chromatisch abwärts bis

TIPS:

✏ The same tips apply here as to no.4, the most important factor again being the unhindered and rapid movement of the foremost part of the tongue, which is evident from the free and open sound of the accentuated note.

✏ The staccato notes should approach the final note without tenseness. In bars 4 and 5, therefore, the beginning of the group of notes must neither come too late nor be accentuated. The only accent is invariably on the last note of each group. One heads for the final note 'with gusto', so to speak.

TIPPS:

✏ Es gelten die gleichen Tipps wie bei Nr. 4; auch hier ist das Wichtigste die freie, schnelle Bewegung des vorderen Zungenteils, die man am freien und offenen Klang der akzentuierten Note erkennt.

✏ Die Staccato-Noten sollen locker auf die Schlussnote zulaufen. Vor allem in den Takten 4 und 5 darf daher der Beginn der Notengruppen weder zu spät sein, noch betont werden. Der einzige Akzent liegt immer auf der Schlussnote jeder Gruppe. Man spielt sozusagen mit Schwung auf die letzte Note zu.

ALTERNATIVES:

1.) Play the exercises in pianissimo and also in forte.
2.) Play the exercises at a markedly slower tempo (♩ = 80 – 88).

VARIANTEN:

1.) Die Übungen im Pianissimo und auch im Forte spielen.
2.) Die Übungen in deutlich langsamerem Tempo spielen (♩ = 80 bis 88).

6. RHYTHMIC EXERCISES

AIM: These exercises are aimed at achieving differentiated and musically shaped articulation.

EXECUTION: Play the following exercises in an easy dynamic (mp or mf) and at a comfortable tempo (♩. = 126 – 138):

6. RHYTHMISCHE ÜBUNGEN

ZIEL: Ziel der Übungen ist eine differenzierte und musikalisch gestaltete Artikulation.

AUSFÜHRUNG: Folgende Übungen in einer entspannten Dynamik (mp oder mf) und in einem angenehmen Tempo (♩. = 126 bis 138) spielen:

chromatically downwards to
chromatisch abwärts bis

TIP:

✏ The accents invariably come at the beginning of the bar. They should not sound heavy but rather like a "bouncing off" from the beginning of the bar. The exercises should flow lightly and not require much effort to play.

ALTERNATIVES:

1.) Play the exercises in pianissimo and also in forte.
2.) Play the exercises at a markedly slower tempo (♩. = ca. 100).
3.) Play the exercises at a very rapid tempo. This is good for developing stamina, but there must be no stiffening up!

TIPP:

✏ Die Betonungen liegen immer auf dem Taktbeginn. Sie sollen nicht als schwer empfunden werden, sondern als ein Abfedern vom Taktanfang. Die Übungen sollen leicht und kraftsparend sein.

VARIANTEN:

1.) Die Übungen im Pianissimo und auch im Forte spielen.
2.) Die Übungen in deutlich langsamerem Tempo spielen (♩. = ca. 100).
3.) Die Übungen in sehr schnellem Tempo spielen. Gut für die Kondition – aber nicht Verkrampfen!

7. RHYTHMIC EXERCISES

AIM: The same aim and tips apply to these exercises as to exercises no. 6.

EXECUTION: Play the following exercises in an easy dynamic (mp or mf) and at a comfortable tempo (♪. = 80 – 84):

7. RHYTHMISCHE ÜBUNGEN

ZIEL: Es gelten für diese Übungen das gleiche Ziel und die gleichen Tipps wie für die Übungen Nr. 6.

AUSFÜHRUNG: Folgende Übungen in einer entspannten Dynamik (mp oder mf) und in einem angenehmen Tempo (♪. = 80 bis 84) spielen:

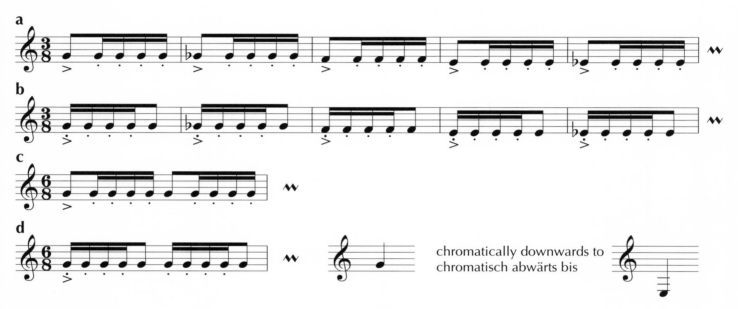

chromatically downwards to
chromatisch abwärts bis

TIP:

✏ The eighth notes should be sonorous but not as broad as a portato.

ALTERNATIVES:

1.) Play the exercise in pianissimo and also in forte.
2.) Play the exercises at a markedly slower tempo (♪. = 69 – 72).

TIPP:

✏ Die Achtel-Noten sollen klangvoll sein, aber nicht so breit wie ein Portato.

VARIANTEN:

1.) Die Übung im Pianissimo und auch im Forte spielen.
2.) Die Übungen in deutlich langsamerem Tempo spielen (♪. = 69 bis 72).

8. SOUND EXERCISE

AIM: The same aims and tips apply to this exercise as to exercise no. 1.

EXECUTION: Play the following exercise in an easy dynamic (mp or mf) and at a quick but not strenuous tempo (♩ = 120 – 126):

8. KLANGÜBUNG

ZIEL: Es gelten für diese Übung die gleichen Ziele und Tipps wie für Übung Nr. 1.

AUSFÜHRUNG: Folgende Übung in einer entspannten Dynamik (mp oder mf) und in einem schnellen, aber nicht angestrengten Tempo (♩ = 120 – 126) spielen:

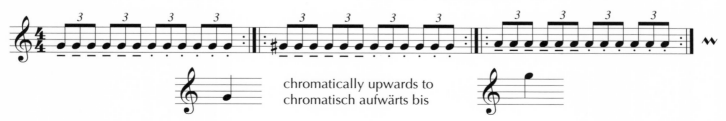

chromatically upwards to
chromatisch aufwärts bis

TIP:

✎ Watch that the tone remains uniform when the difficult change of registers is being negotiated. With an awareness for tone production and breath control, the b♭ and b can have approximately the same fullness yet also speak equally cleanly! However, this does not work with bad or mediocre reeds and requires considerable care when practising!

ALTERNATIVES:

1.) Play the exercise in pianissimo and also in forte.
2.) Play the exercise at a markedly slower tempo (♩ = 88 – 96)

TIPP:

✎ Man achte auf den klanglichen Ausgleich beim schwierigen Registerwechsel. Bewusste Klangformung und Luftführung können erreichen, dass b' und h' sowohl ähnlich voll klingen als auch gleich sauber ansprechen! Dies gelingt jedoch nicht mit schlechten oder mittelmäßigen Blättern und erfordert große Sorgfalt beim Üben!

VARIANTEN:

1.) Die Übung im Pianissimo und auch im Forte spielen.
2.) Die Übung in deutlich langsamerem Tempo spielen (♩ = 88 bis 96):

9. SOUND EXERCISE

AIM, EXECUTION and **TIPS**
as in exercise no. 2 (♩ = 116 – 120):

9. KLANGÜBUNG

ZIEL, AUSFÜHRUNG und **TIPPS**
wie bei Übung Nr. 2 (♩ = 116 bis 120):

chromatically upwards to
chromatisch aufwärts bis

ALTERNATIVES:

1.) Play the exercises in pianissimo and also in forte.
2.) Play the exercises at a markedly slower tempo (♩ = 80 – 88).
3.) Play the exercises at a very rapid tempo (stamina training!)

VARIANTEN:

1.) Die Übungen im Pianissimo und auch im Forte spielen.
2.) Die Übungen in deutlich langsamerem Tempo spielen (♩ = 80 bis 88).
3. Die Übungen in sehr schnellem Tempo spielen (Konditionstraining!).

10. SOUND EXERCISE

AIM, EXECUTION and **TIPS**
as in exercise no. 3 (♩ = 116 – 120):

10. KLANGÜBUNG

ZIEL, AUSFÜHRUNG und **TIPPS**
wie bei Übung Nr. 3 (♩ = 116 bis 120):

a

b

c

d

chromatically upwards to
chromatisch aufwärts bis

ALTERNATIVES:

1.) Play the exercises in pianissimo and also in forte.
2.) Play the exercises at a markedly slower tempo (♩ = 80 – 88).
3.) Play the exercises at a very rapid tempo (stamina training!)

VARIANTEN:

1.) Die Übungen im Pianissimo und auch im Forte spielen.
2.) Die Übungen in deutlich langsamerem Tempo spielen (♩ = 80 bis 88).
3.) Die Übungen in sehr schnellem Tempo spielen (Konditionstraining!).

11. LOOSENING-UP EXERCISES

AIM, EXECUTION and **TIPS**
as in exercise no. 4 (♩ = 112 – 120):

11. LOCKERUNGSÜBUNGEN

ZIEL, AUSFÜHRUNG und **TIPPS**
wie bei Übung Nr. 4 (♩ = 112 bis 120):

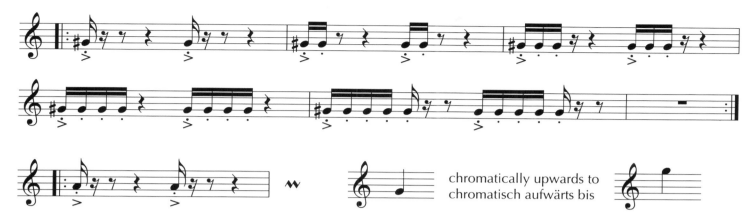

ALTERNATIVES:

1.) Play the exercises in pianissimo and also in forte.
2.) Play the exercises at a markedly slower tempo (♩ = 80 – 88).

VARIANTEN:

1.) Die Übungen im Pianissimo und auch im Forte spielen.
2.) Die Übungen in deutlich langsamerem Tempo spielen (♩ = 80 bis 88).

12. LOOSENING-UP EXERCISES

AIM, EXECUTION and **TIPS**
as in exercises no. 5 (♩ = 112 – 120):

12. LOCKERUNGSÜBUNGEN

ZIEL, AUSFÜHRUNG und **TIPPS**
wie bei den Übungen Nr. 5 (♩ = 112 bis 120):

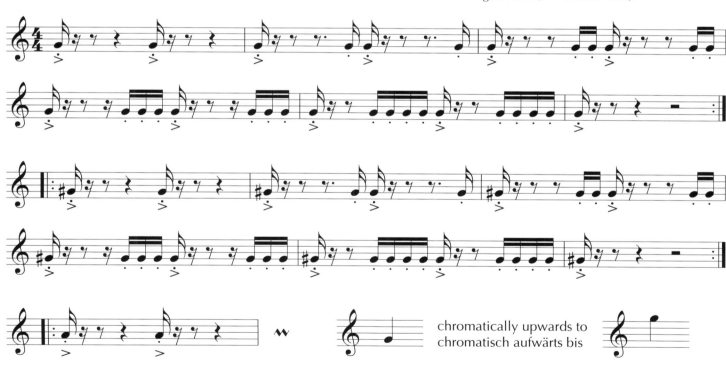

ALTERNATIVES:

1.) Play the exercises in pianissimo and also in forte.
2.) Play the exercises at a markedly slower tempo (♩ = 80 – 88).

VARIANTEN:

1.) Die Übungen im Pianissimo und auch im Forte spielen.
2.) Die Übungen in deutlich langsamerem Tempo spielen (♩ = 80 bis 88).

13. RHYTHMIC EXERCISES

AIM, EXECUTION and **TIPS**
as in exercises no. 6 (♩. = 126 – 138):

chromatically upwards to
chromatisch aufwärts bis

ALTERNATIVES:

1.) Play the exercises in pianissimo and also in forte.
2.) Play the exercises at a markedly slower tempo
    (♩. = ca. 100).

13. RHYTHMISCHE ÜBUNGEN

ZIEL, AUSFÜHRUNG und **TIPPS**
wie bei den Übungen Nr. 6 (♩. = 126 bis 138):

VARIANTEN:

1.) Die Übungen im Pianissimo und auch im Forte spielen.
2.) Die Übungen in deutlich langsamerem Tempo spielen
    (♩. = ca. 100).

14. RHYTHMIC EXERCISES

AIM, EXECUTION and **TIPS**
as in exercises no. 7 (♩. = 80 – 84):

14. RHYTHMISCHE ÜBUNGEN

ZIEL, AUSFÜHRUNG und **TIPPS**
wie bei den Übungen Nr. 7 (♩. = 80 bis 84):

a

b

c

d

chromatically upwards to
chromatisch aufwärts bis

ALTERNATIVES:

1.) Play the exercises in pianissimo and also in forte.
2.) Play the exercises at a markedly slower tempo
(♩. = 69 – 72)

VARIANTEN:

1.) Die Übungen im Pianissimo und auch im Forte spielen.
2.) Die Übungen in deutlich langsamerem Tempo spielen
(♩. = 69 bis 72).

15. SOUND EXERCISE

AIM, EXECUTION and **TIPS**
as in exercise no. 1 (♩ = 120 – 126):

15. KLANGÜBUNG

ZIEL, AUSFÜHRUNG und **TIPPS**
wie bei der Übung Nr. 1 (♩ = 120 bis 126):

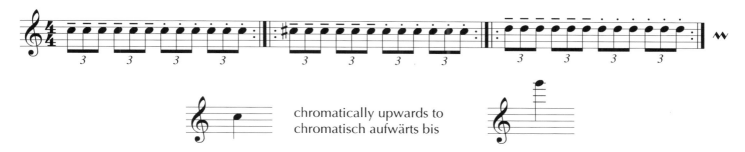

chromatically upwards to
chromatisch aufwärts bis

ALTERNATIVES:

1.) Play the exercise in pianissimo and also in forte.
2.) Play the exercise at a markedly slower tempo
(♩ = 88 – 96).

VARIANTEN:

1.) Die Übung im Pianissimo und auch im Forte spielen.
2.) Die Übung in deutlich langsamerem Tempo spielen
(♩ = 88 bis 96).

16. SOUND EXERCISES

AIM, EXECUTION and **TIPS**
as in exercises no. 2 (♩ = 116 – 120):

16. KLANGÜBUNGEN

ZIEL, AUSFÜHRUNG und **TIPPS**
wie bei den Übungen Nr. 2 (♩ = 116 bis 120):

a

b

c

d

chromatically upwards to
chromatisch aufwärts bis

ALTERNATIVES:

1.) Play the exercises in pianissimo and also in forte.
2.) Play the exercises at a markedly slower tempo (♩ = 80 – 88).
3.) Play the exercises at a very rapid tempo. The exercises **c** and **d** are then very hard work (no tensing up!). They are thus well suited to building up stamina.

VARIANTEN:

1.) Die Übungen im Pianissimo und auch im Forte spielen.
2.) Die Übungen in deutlich langsamerem Tempo spielen (♩ = 80 bis 88).
3.) Die Übungen in sehr schnellem Tempo spielen. Die Übungen **c** und **d** kosten dann doch viel Kraft (locker bleiben!). Sie eignen sich auch zum Training der Kondition.

17. SOUND EXERCISES

AIM, EXECUTION and **TIPS**
as in exercises no. 3 (♩ = 116 – 120):

17. KLANGÜBUNGEN

ZIEL, AUSFÜHRUNG und **TIPPS**
wie bei den Übungen Nr. 3 (♩ = 116 bis 120):

a

b

c

d

chromatically upwards to
chromatisch aufwärts bis

ALTERNATIVES:

1.) Play the exercises in pianissimo and also in forte.
2.) Play the exercises at a markedly slower tempo
   (♩ = 80 – 88).
3.) Play the exercises at a very rapid tempo.

VARIANTEN:

1.) Die Übungen im Pianissimo und auch im Forte spielen.
2.) die Übungen in deutlich langsamerem Tempo spielen
   (♩ = 80 bis 88).
3.) Die Übungen in sehr schnellem Tempo spielen.

18. LOOSENING-UP EXERCISES

AIM, EXECUTION and **TIPS**
as in exercises no. 4 (♩ = 112 – 120):

18. LOCKERUNGSÜBUNGEN

ZIEL, AUSFÜHRUNG und **TIPPS**
wie bei den Übungen Nr. 4 (♩ = 112 bis 120):

chromatically upwards to
chromatisch aufwärts bis

ALTERNATIVES:

1.) Play the exercises in pianissimo and also in forte.
2.) Play the exercises at a markedly slower tempo
   (♩ = 80 – 88).

VARIANTEN:

1.) Die Übungen im Pianissimo und auch im Forte spielen.
2.) Die Übungen in deutlich langsamerem Tempo spielen
   (♩ = 80 bis 88).

19. LOOSENING-UP EXERCISES

AIM, EXECUTION and **TIPS**
as in exercises no. 5 (♩ = 112 – 120):

19. LOCKERUNGSÜBUNGEN

ZIEL, AUSFÜHRUNG und **TIPPS**
wie bei den Übungen Nr. 5 (♩ = 112 bis 120):

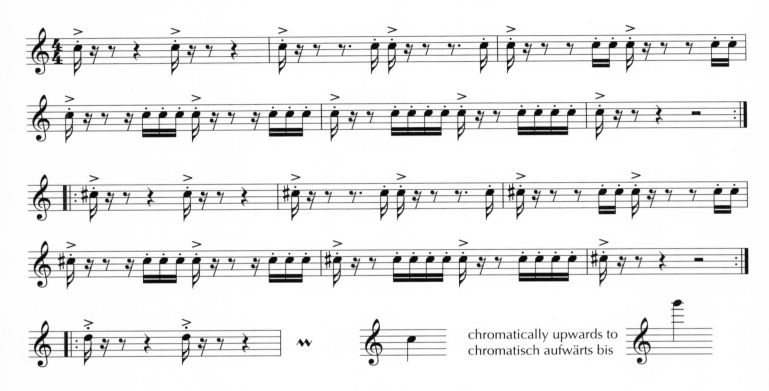

chromatically upwards to
chromatisch aufwärts bis

ALTERNATIVES:

1.) Play the exercises in pianissimo and also in forte.
2.) Play the exercises at a markedly slower tempo
(♩ = 80 – 88).

VARIANTEN:

1.) Die Übungen im Pianissimo und auch im Forte spielen.
2.) Die Übungen in deutlich langsamerem Tempo spielen
(♩ = 80 bis 88).

20: RHYTHMIC EXERCISES

AIM, EXECUTION and **TIPS**
as in exercises no. 6 (♩. = 126 – 138):

20. RHYTHMISCHE ÜBUNGEN

ZIEL, AUSFÜHRUNG und **TIPPS**
wie bei den Übungen Nr. 6 (♩. = 126 bis 138):

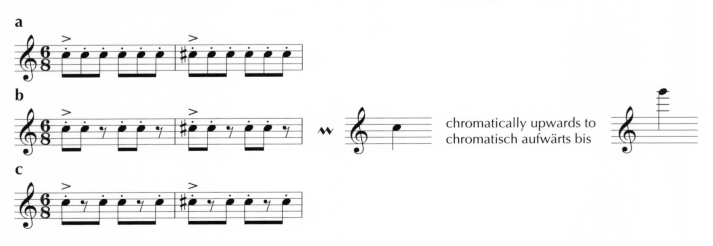

chromatically upwards to
chromatisch aufwärts bis

ALTERNATIVES:

1.) Play the exercises in pianissimo and also in forte.
2.) Play the exercises at a markedly slower tempo
(♩. = ca. 100).

VARIANTEN:

1.) Die Übungen im Pianissimo und auch im Forte spielen.
2.) Die Übungen in deutlich langsamerem Tempo spielen
(♩. = ca. 100).

21. RHYTHMIC EXERCISES

AIM, EXECUTION and **TIPS**
as in exercises no. 7 (♩. = 80 – 84):

21. RHYTHMISCHE ÜBUNGEN

ZIEL, AUSFÜHRUNG und **TIPPS**
wie bei den Übungen Nr. 7 (♩. = 80 bis 84):

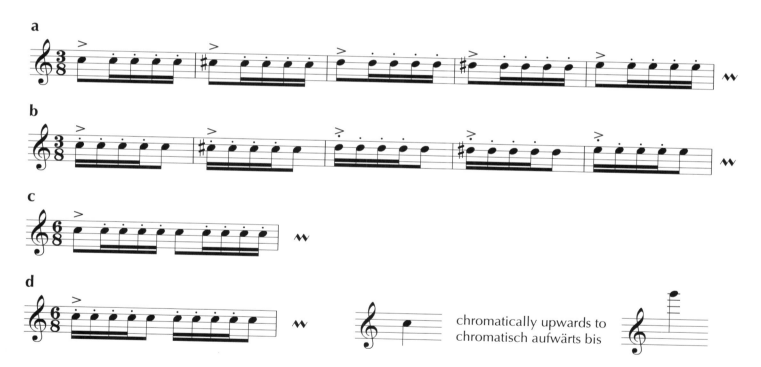

chromatically upwards to
chromatisch aufwärts bis

ALTERNATIVES:

1.) Play the exercises in pianissimo and also in forte.
2.) Play the exercises at a markedly slower tempo
(♩. = 69 – 72).

VARIANTEN:

1.) Die Übungen im Pianissimo und auch im Forte spielen.
2.) Die Übungen in deutlich langsamerem Tempo spielen
(♩. = 69 bis 72).

22. COORDINATION EXERCISE

AIM: The tongue attack and fingerwork must be aligned with absolutely precision. The goal here is to practise this in short sequences of notes and scale segments that are easy to finger.

EXECUTION: Play the following exercise in an easy dynamic (mp or mf) and at a comfortable tempo (♩ = 112 – 120):

22. KOORDINATIONSÜBUNG

ZIEL: Zungenstoß und Greifbewegung müssen absolut präzise zusammenpassen. Dies soll in kurzen Notenfolgen und einfach zu greifenden Skalen geübt werden.

AUSFÜHRUNG: Folgende Übung in einer entspannten Dynamik (mp oder mf) und in einem angenehmen Tempo (♩ = 112 bis 120) spielen:

TIPS:

✏ All tips for the loosening-up exercise no. 4 apply here too.

✏ For monitoring purposes, and especially if problems arise in the coordination of tongue and fingers, also play the exercise legato.

✏ Relaxing the tongue/throat region can only succeed if the fingerwork is also free of tenseness .

ALTERNATIVES:

1.) Play the exercise in pianissimo and also in forte.
2.) Play the exercise at a markedly slower tempo (♩ = 80 – 88).

TIPPS:

✏ Es gelten alle Tipps der Lockerungsübung Nr. 4.

✏ Zur Kontrolle – und vor allem, wenn sich beim Zusammenspiel von Zunge und Fingern Schwierigkeiten ergeben – die Übung auch im Legato spielen.

✏ Das Entspannen des Zungen-/Rachenbereichs kann nur gelingen, wenn auch die Finger entspannt greifen.

VARIANTEN:

1.) Die Übung im Pianissimo und auch im Forte spielen.
2.) Die Übung in deutlich langsamerem Tempo (♩ = 80 bis 88) spielen.

23. COORDINATION EXERCISE

AIM: Again, this exercise is aimed at improving the synchronisation of fingers and tongue.

EXECUTION: Play the following exercise in an easy dynamic (mf or mp) and at a comfortable tempo (♩ = 112 – 120):

23. KOORDINATIONSÜBUNG

ZIEL: Auch diese Übung dient der Synchronisation von Fingern und Zunge.

AUSFÜHRUNG: Folgende Übung in einer entspannten Dynamik (mf oder mp) und in einem angenehmen Tempo (♩ = 112 –120) spielen:

TIPS:

- All tips for the loosening-up exercise no. 5 apply.

- Here, too, practising the exercise in legato is advisable for monitoring and in the event of problems arising.

- It frequently happens that the player comes in too late in bars 4 and 5. Playing lightly 'towards' the accentuated principal note makes coming in on time much easier.

- Relaxation and momentum are helpful here, too.

ALTERNATIVES:

1.) Play the exercise in pianissimo and also in forte.
2.) Play the exercise at a markedly slower tempo (♩ = 80 – 88).

TIPPS:

- Es gelten alle Tipps der Lockerungsübung Nr. 5.

- Auch hier empfiehlt sich zur Kontrolle und bei Schwierigkeiten ein Üben im Legato.

- In den Takten vier und fünf passiert es häufig, dass man zu spät einsetzt. Ein lockeres Hinspielen auf den Akzent der Hauptnote erleichtert sehr ein pünktliches Einsetzen.

- Auch hier hilft Lockerheit und Schwung.

VARIANTEN:

1.) Die Übung im Pianissimo und auch im Forte spielen.
2.) Die Übung in deutlich langsamerem Tempo spielen (♩ = 80 bis 88).

24. COORDINATION EXERCISE

EXECUTION: Practise the same exercise as no. 22 using the following scale segments:

24. KOORDINATIONSÜBUNG

AUSFÜHRUNG: Die gleiche Übung wie bei Nr. 22 in folgenden Skalenabschnitten üben:

C major / C-Dur

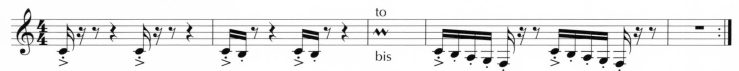

F major / F-Dur

C major / C-Dur

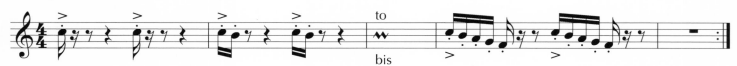

F major / F-Dur

G major / G-Dur

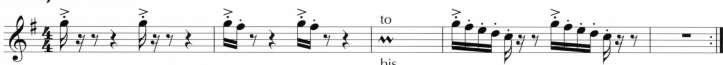

C major / C-Dur

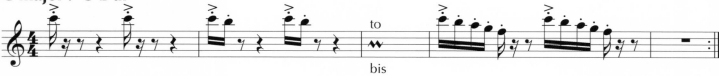

25. COORDINATION EXERCISE

EXECUTION: Practise the same exercise as no. 23 using the following scale segments:

25. KOORDINATIONSÜBUNG

AUSFÜHRUNG: Die gleiche Übung wie bei Nr. 23 in folgenden Skalenabschnitten üben:

C major / C-Dur

F major / F-Dur

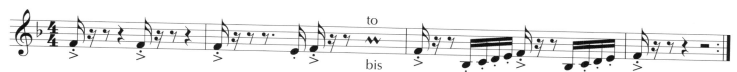

C major / C-Dur

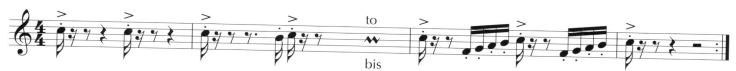

F major / F-Dur

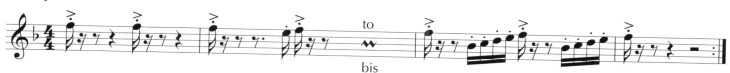

G major / G-Dur

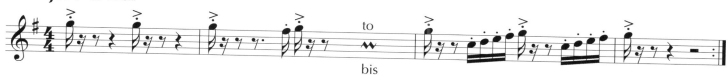

C major / C-Dur

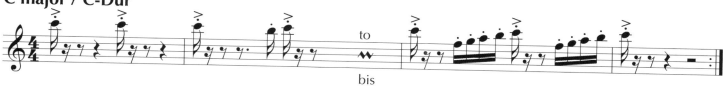

26. COORDINATION EXERCISE

EXECUTION: Practise the same exercise as no. 22 using the following scale segments:

26. KOORDINATIONSÜBUNG

AUSFÜHRUNG: Die gleiche Übung wie bei Nr. 22 in folgenden Skalen abschnitten üben:

D major / D-Dur

D minor / d-Moll

G minor / g-Moll

A minor / a-Moll

B♭ major / B-Dur

D major / D-Dur

D minor / d-Moll

G minor / g-Moll

A minor / a-Moll

B♭ major / B-Dur

27. COORDINATION EXERCISE

EXECUTION: Practise the same exercise as no. 23 using the following scale segments:

27. KOORDINATIONSÜBUNG

AUSFÜHRUNG: Die gleiche Übung wie bei Nr. 23 in folgenden Skalenabschnitten üben:

D major / D-Dur

D minor / d-Moll

G minor / g-Moll

A minor / a-Moll

B♭ major / B-Dur

D major / D-Dur

D minor / d-Moll

G minor / g-Moll

A minor / a-Moll

B♭ major / B-Dur

28. COORDINATION EXERCISE

EXECUTION: Practise the same exercises as no. 22 using the following scale segments:

28. KOORDINATIONSÜBUNG

AUSFÜHRUNG: Die gleiche Übungen wie bei Nr. 22 in folgenden Skalenabschnitten üben:

C minor / c-Moll

E♭ major / Es-Dur

E minor / e-Moll

A major / A-Dur

C minor / c-Moll

E♭ major / Es-Dur

E minor / e-Moll

A major / A-Dur

C minor / c-Moll

29. COORDINATION EXERCISE

EXECUTION: Practise the same exercise as no. 23 using the following scale segments:

29. KOORDINATIONSÜBUNG

AUSFÜHRUNG: Die gleiche Übung wie bei Nr. 23 in folgenden Skalenabschnitten üben:

30. COORDINATION EXERCISE

EXECUTION: Practise the same exercise as no. 22 using the following scale segments:

30. KOORDINATIONSÜBUNG

AUSFÜHRUNG: Die gleiche Übung wie bei Nr. 22 in folgenden Skalenabschnitten üben:

B major / H-Dur

E major / E-Dur

F minor / f-Moll

A♭ major / As-Dur

B major / H-Dur

E major / E-Dur

F minor / f-Moll

A♭ major / As-Dur

B major / H-Dur

31. COORDINATION EXERCISE

EXECUTION: Practise the same exercise as no. 23 using the following scale segments:

31. KOORDINATIONSÜBUNG

AUSFÜHRUNG: Die gleiche Übung wie bei Nr. 23 in folgenden Skalenabschnitten üben:

B major / H-Dur

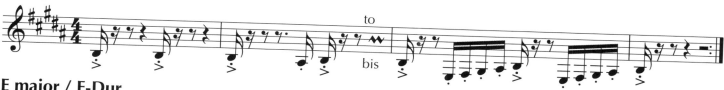

E major / E-Dur

F minor / f-Moll

A♭ major / As-Dur

B major / H-Dur

E major / E-Dur

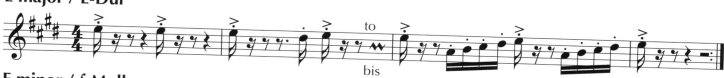

F minor / f-Moll

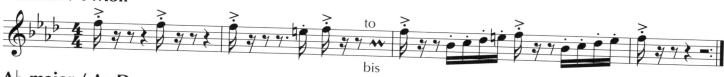

A♭ major / As-Dur

B major / H-Dur

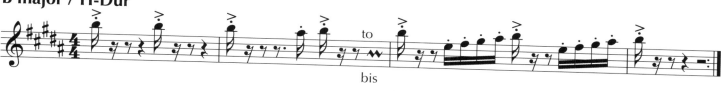

32. COORDINATION EXERCISE

EXECUTION: Practise the same exercise as no. 22 using the following scale segments:

32. KOORDINATIONSÜBUNG

AUSFÜHRUNG: Die gleiche Übung wie bei Nr. 22 in folgenden Skalenabschnitten üben:

Db major / Des-Dur

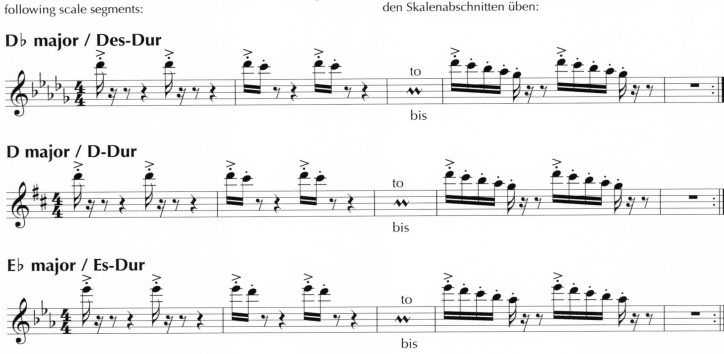

D major / D-Dur

Eb major / Es-Dur

C# minor /cis-Moll

D minor / d-Moll

Eb minor / es-Moll

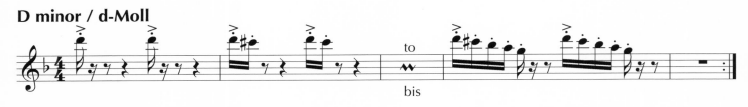

33. COORDINATION EXERCISE

EXECUTION: Practise the same exercise as no. 23 using the following scale segments:

33. KOORDINATIONSÜBUNG

AUSFÜHRUNG: Die gleiche Übung wie bei Nr. 23 in folgenden Skalenabschnitten üben:

D♭ major / Des-Dur

D major / D-Dur

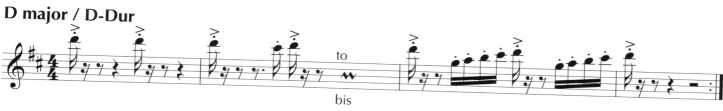

E♭ major / Es-Dur

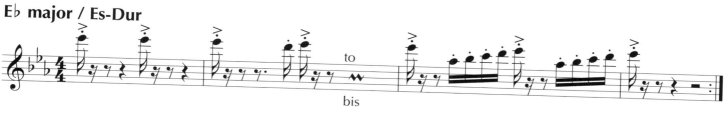

C♯ minor / cis-Moll

D minor / d-Moll

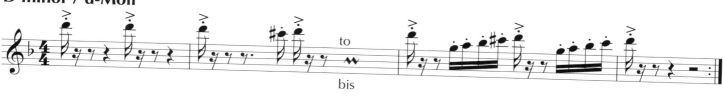

E♭ minor / es-Moll

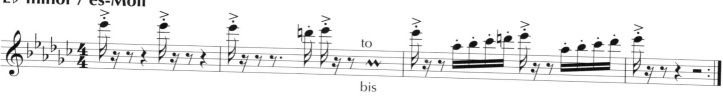

34. COORDINATION EXERCISE

EXECUTION: Practise the same exercise as no. 22 using the following scale segments:

34. KOORDINATIONSÜBUNG

AUSFÜHRUNG: Die gleiche Übung wie bei Nr. 22 in folgenden Skalenabschnitten üben:

E major / E-Dur

F major / F-Dur

F♯ major / Fis-Dur

E minor / e-Moll

F minor / f-Moll

F♯ minor / fis-Moll

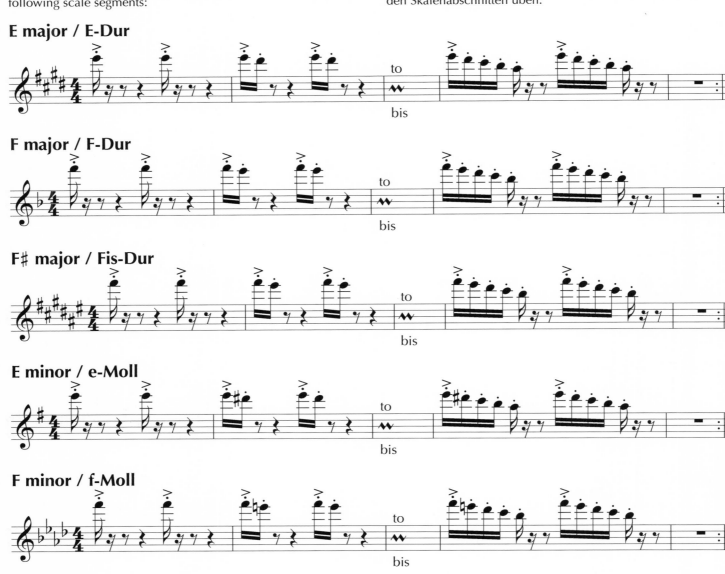

35. COORDINATION EXERCISE

EXECUTION: Practise the same exercise as no. 23 using the following scale segments:

35. KOORDINATIONSÜBUNG

AUSFÜHRUNG: Die gleiche Übung wie bei Nr. 23 in folgenden Skalen

E major / E-Dur

to
bis

F major / F-Dur

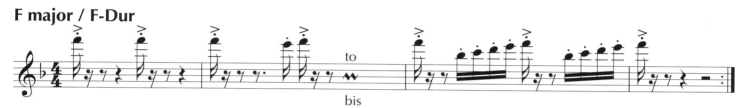

to
bis

F♯ major / Fis-Dur

to
bis

E minor / e-Moll

to
bis

F minor / f-Moll

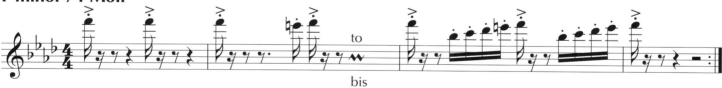

to
bis

F♯ minor / fis-Moll

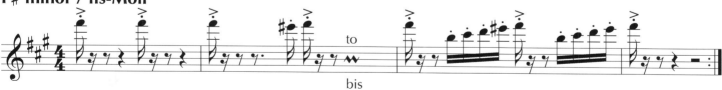

to
bis

36. RESPONSE AND COORDINATION EXERCISE:

AIM: Here, too, the objective is to practise coordination of the tongue with the fingers. But the extra difficulty presented by arpeggios is the widely differing response of notes in the different registers.

EXECUTION: Play the following exercise in an easy dynamic (mp or mf) and at a calm tempo (♩ = 112 – 120):

36. ANSPRACHE UND KOORDINATIONSÜBUNG

ZIEL: Auch hier soll die Koordination zwischen Zunge und Fingern geübt werden. Die zusätzliche Schwierigkeit bei Dreiklängen besteht aber in der sehr unterschiedlichen Ansprache der Töne in den verschiedenen Registern.

AUSFÜHRUNG: Folgende Übung in einer entspannten Dynamik (mp oder mf) und in einem ruhigen Tempo (♩ = 112 bis 120) spielen:

TIPS:

- All tips for the loosening-up exercise no. 4 apply here.

- Check that there is no tenseness by playing it legato first.

- Even when playing notes that do not speak easily, the fingers must remain supple.

ALTERNATIVES:

1.) Play the exercise in pianissimo and also in forte.
2.) Vary the tempo

TIPPS:

- Es gelten alle Tipps der Lockerungsübung Nr. 4.

- Die Übung zuerst im Legato auf Lockerheit kontrollieren.

- Auch wenn die Töne schwerer ansprechen muss man mit den Fingern entspannt bleiben.

VARIANTEN:

1.) Die Übung im Pianissimo und auch im Forte spielen.
2.) Das Tempo variieren

37. RESPONSE AND COORDINATION EXERCISE:

AIM and **EXECUTION**
as in exercise 36 (♩ = 112 – 120):

37. ANSPRACHE UND KOORDINATIONSÜBUNG

ZIEL und **AUSFÜHRUNG**
wie bei Übung Nr. 36 (♩ = 112 bis 120):

TIP:

- All tips for exercises no. 5 and no. 36 apply here.

ALTERNATIVES:

1.) Play the exercise in pianissimo and also in forte.
2.) Vary the tempo

TIPP:

- Es gelten alle Tipps der Übungen Nr. 5 und Nr. 36.

VARIANTEN:

1.) Die Übung im Pianissimo und auch im Forte spielen.
2.) Das Tempo variieren

38. RESPONSE AND COORDINATION EXERCISE

EXECUTION: Practise the same exercise as no. 36 on the following arpeggios:

38. ANSPRACHE UND KOORDINATIONSÜBUNG

AUSFÜHRUNG: Die gleiche Übung wie bei Nr. 36 in folgenden Dreiklängen üben:

A♭ major / As-Dur

A major / A-Dur

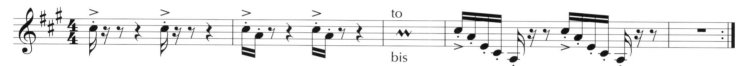

B♭ major / B-Dur

G♯ minor / gis-Moll

A minor / a-Moll

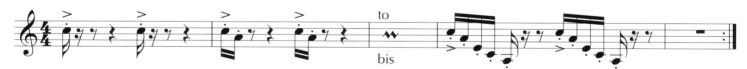

B♭ minor / b-Moll

39. RESPONSE AND COORDINATION EXERCISE

EXECUTION: Practise the same exercise as no. 37 on the following arpeggios:

39. ANSPRACHE UND KOORDINATIONSÜBUNG

AUSFÜHRUNG: Die gleiche Übung wie bei Nr. 37 in folgenden Dreiklängen üben:

A♭ major / As-Dur

A major / A-Dur

B♭ major / B-Dur

G♯ minor / gis-Moll

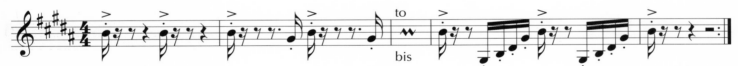

A minor / a-Moll

B♭ minor / b-Moll

40. RESPONSE AND COORDINATION EXERCISE

EXECUTION: Practise the same exercise as no. 36 on the following arpeggios:

40. ANSPRACHE UND KOORDINATIONSÜBUNG

AUSFÜHRUNG: Die gleiche Übung wie bei Nr. 36 in folgenden Dreiklängen üben:

B major / H-Dur

C major / C-Dur

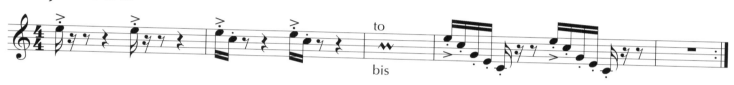

D♭ major / Des-Dur

B minor / h-Moll

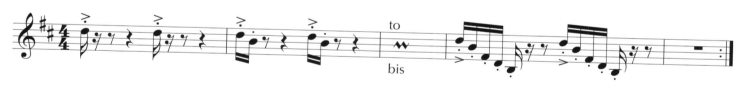

C minor / c-Moll

C# minor / cis-Moll

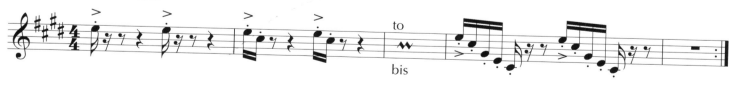

41. RESPONSE AND COORDINATION EXERCISE

EXECUTION: Practise the same exercise as no. 37 on the following arpeggios:

41. ANSPRACHE UND KOORDINATIONSÜBUNG

AUSFÜHRUNG: Die gleiche Übung wie bei Nr. 37 in folgenden Dreiklängen üben:

B major / H-Dur

C major / C-Dur

D♭ major / Des-Dur

B minor / h-Moll

C minor / c-Moll

C♯ minor / cis-Moll

42. RESPONSE AND COORDINATION EXERCISE

EXECUTION: Practise the same exercise as no. 36 on the following arpeggios:

42. ANSPRACHE UND KOORDINATIONSÜBUNG

AUSFÜHRUNG: Die gleiche Übung wie bei Nr. 36 in folgenden Dreiklängen üben:

D major / D-Dur

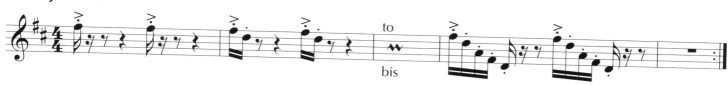

E♭ major / Es-Dur

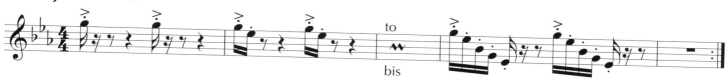

E major / E-Dur

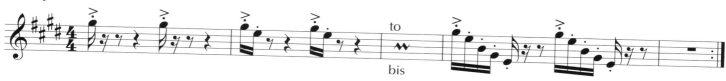

D minor / d-Moll

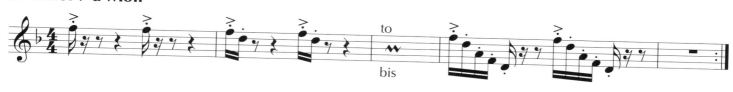

D♯ minor / dis-Moll

E minor / e-Moll

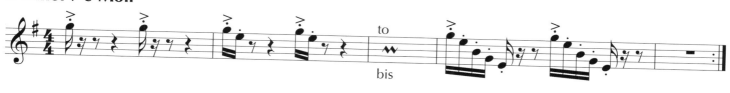

43. RESPONSE AND COORDINATION EXERCISE

EXECUTION: Practise the same exercise as no. 37 on the following arpeggios:

43. ANSPRACHE UND KOORDINATIONSÜBUNG

AUSFÜHRUNG: Die gleiche Übung wie bei Nr. 37 in folgenden Dreiklängen üben:

D major / D-Dur

Eb major / Es-Dur

E major / E-Dur

D minor / d-Moll

D# minor / dis-Moll

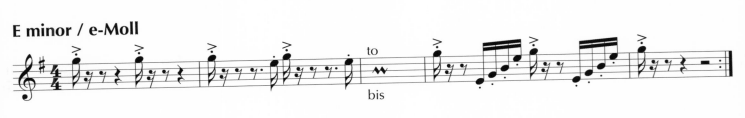

E minor / e-Moll

44. RESPONSE AND COORDINATION EXERCISE

EXECUTION: Practise the same exercise as no. 36 on the following arpeggios:

44. ANSPRACHE UND KOORDINATIONSÜBUNG

AUSFÜHRUNG: Die gleiche Übung wie bei Nr. 36 in folgenden Dreiklängen üben:

F major / F-Dur

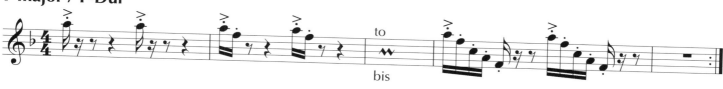

F♯ major / Fis-Dur

G major / G-Dur

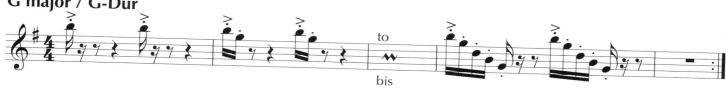

F minor / f-Moll

F♯ minor / fis-Moll

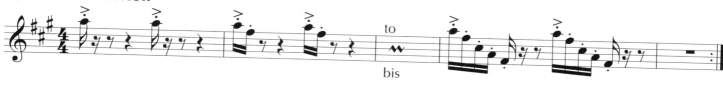

G minor / g-Moll

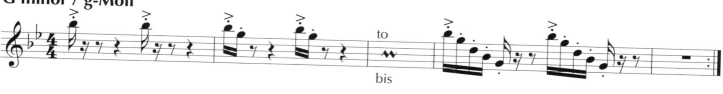

45. RESPONSE AND COORDINATION EXERCISE

EXECUTION: Practise the same exercise as no. 37 on the following arpeggios:

45. ANSPRACHE UND KOORDINATIONSÜBUNG

AUSFÜHRUNG: Die gleiche Übung wie bei Nr. 37 in folgenden Dreiklängen üben:

F major / F-Dur

F# major / Fis-Dur

G major / G-Dur

F minor / f-Moll

F# minor / fis-Moll

G minor / g-Moll

46. RESPONSE AND COORDINATION EXERCISE

EXECUTION: Practise the same exercise as no. 36 on the following arpeggios:

46. ANSPRACHE UND KOORDINATIONSÜBUNG

AUSFÜHRUNG: Die gleiche Übung wie bei Nr. 36 in folgenden Dreiklängen üben:

A♭ major / As-Dur

A major / A-Dur

B♭ major / B-Dur

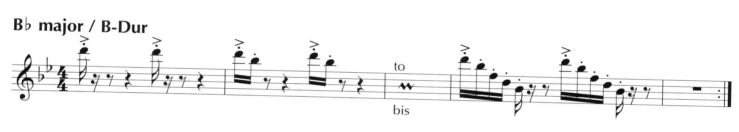

G♯ minor / gis-Moll

A minor / a-Moll

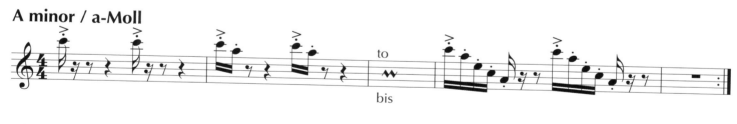

B♭ minor / b-Moll

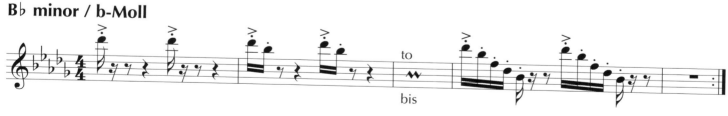

47. RESPONSE AND COORDINATION EXERCISE

EXECUTION: Practise the same exercise as no. 37 on the following arpeggios:

47. ANSPRACHE UND KOORDINATIONSÜBUNG

AUSFÜHRUNG: Die gleiche Übung wie bei Nr. 37 in folgenden Dreiklängen üben:

A♭ major / As-Dur

A major / A-Dur

B♭ major / B-Dur

G♯ minor / gis-Moll

A minor / a-Moll

B♭ minor / b-Moll

48. RESPONSE AND COORDINATION EXERCISE

EXECUTION: Practise the same exercise as no. 36 on the following arpeggios:

48. ANSPRACHE UND KOORDINATIONSÜBUNG

AUSFÜHRUNG: Die gleiche Übung wie bei Nr. 36 in folgenden Dreiklängen üben:

B major / H-Dur

C major / C-Dur

D♭ major / Des-Dur

B minor / h-Moll

C minor / c-Moll

C# minor / cis-Moll

49. RESPONSE AND COORDINATION EXERCISE

EXECUTION: Practise the same exercise as no. 37 on the following arpeggios:

49. ANSPRACHE UND KOORDINATIONSÜBUNG

AUSFÜHRUNG: Die gleiche Übung wie bei Nr. 37 in folgenden Dreiklängen üben:

B major / H-Dur

C major / C-Dur

Db major / Des-Dur

B minor / h-Moll

C minor / c-Moll

C# minor / cis-Moll

50. STAMINA EXERCISE

AIM: This exercise is designed to train the stamina of the tongue.

EXECUTION: Begin practising the following exercise in a medium dynamic; later on, play it also in forte and in pianissimo:

50. KONDITIONSÜBUNG

ZIEL: Mit dieser Übung soll die Ausdauer der Zunge trainiert werden.

AUSFÜHRUNG: Zunächst in mittlerer Dynamik, später auch im Forte und im Pianissimo folgende Übung spielen:

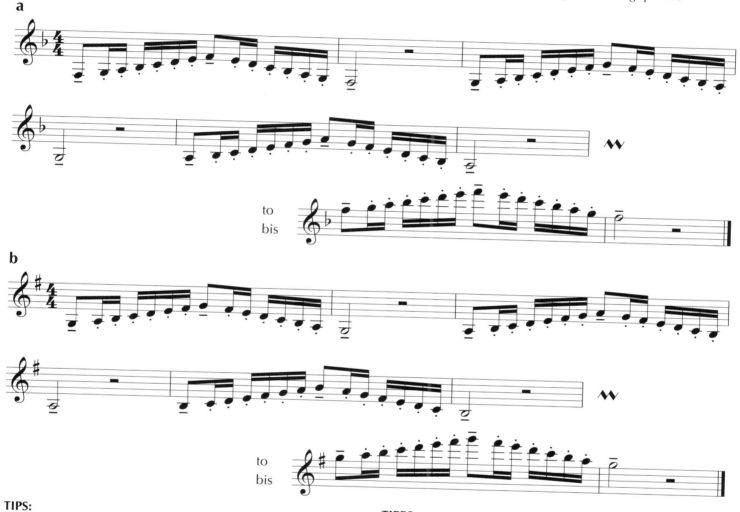

TIPS:

☞ The tempo is to be chosen so that the whole exercise can be managed at the starting speed.

☞ Even in exercises for stamina training, staying relaxed is a priority. But after a certain period the tongue tires, at which point one should leave off practising this exercise. The better strategy is to practise it for shorter periods, but at frequent intervals.

☞ As this exercise deals with fitness, straightforward keys have been chosen. With the Boehm System, F major is simpler, but with the Oehler System, G major. Other keys may also be selected, however.

TIPPS:

☞ Das Tempo der Übung sollte so gewählt werden, dass man die ganze Übung im Anfangstempo schafft.

☞ Auch bei Konditionsübungen steht die Lockerheit im Vordergrund. Nach einer gewissen Zeit ermüdet aber die Zunge. Dann sollte man die Übung nicht länger weiter-üben. Besser ist, die Übung nicht sehr lange, sondern öfters zu üben.

☞ Da es um die Kondition geht, sind einfache Tonarten gewählt worden. Beim Boehm-System ist F-Dur einfacher, beim Oehler-System G-Dur. Es können aber auch andere Tonarten für die Konditionsübung gewählt werden.

51. STAMINA EXERCISE

AIM: This picks up where exercise no. 50 left off, taking it further for stamina training.

EXECUTION: Begin practising the following exercise in a medium dynamic; later, play it also in forte and in pianissimo:

51. KONDITIONSÜBUNG

ZIEL: Eine Steigerung der Übung Nr. 50 zum Training der Ausdauer.

AUSFÜHRUNG: Zunächst in mittlerer Dynamik, später auch im Forte und im Pianissimo folgende Übung spielen:

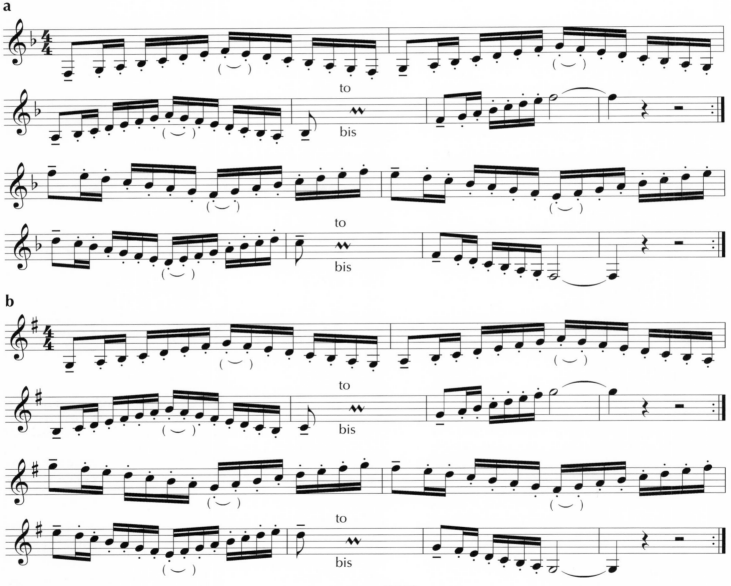

TIPS:

✎ Here, too, the tempo should be chosen so that the tongue has sufficient stamina to keep it up throughout the entire exercise. Breaths may, of course, be taken as necessary.

✎ Initially, the exercise can be made easier by slurring the first two notes on the third beat of the bar.

✎ Here again, for purposes of boosting fitness, it makes sense to choose the simple keys, but others are also possible.

TIPPS:

✎ Auch hier sollte das Tempo so gewählt sein, dass man von der Kondition der Zunge her die ganze Übung darin schafft. Natürlich darf man aber zwischendurch nachatmen.

✎ Man kann die Übung zunächst erleichtern, indem man auf dem dritten Viertel eine Zweier-Bindung einfügt.

✎ Auch hier sind zum Training der Kondition die einfachen Tonarten sinnvoll, aber andere Tonarten ebenfalls möglich.

52. EXERCISES FOR DOUBLE TONGUING

AIM: An introduction to the technique of double tonguing.

EXECUTION: At first, play the following exercises at a relatively slow tempo:

52. ÜBUNGEN FÜR DIE DOPPELZUNGE

ZIEL: Der Einstieg in die Technik der Doppelzunge.

AUSFÜHRUNG: Zunächst in relativ langsamen Tempo folgende Übungen spielen:

TIPS:

- The syllables used for double tonguing consist of "ta" and "ka" (or, if this works better, "te" and "ke"). However, the clarinet speaks very differently on these two different syllables. Careful attention should therefore be given that from the very first exercise onwards, the "ka" (or "ke") speaks quickly and directly. A very relaxed and clearly defined "k" has to be formed for this to succeed. The process is greatly facilitated by playing on a reed that is not too hard.

- This type of staccato seems highly unfamiliar at first. But persevere! It does not take long to learn!

- If the exercise is going well, the tempo may be raised and the dynamics also varied.

TIPPS:

- Die Tonsilben für die Doppelzunge bestehen aus „ta" und „ka" (oder, falls dies besser gehen sollte , aus „te" und „ke"). Die Klarinette spricht auf den beiden unterschiedlichen Silben aber sehr verschieden an. Von dieser ersten Übung an sollte daher darauf geachtet werden, dass das „ka" (bzw. das „ke") schnell und direkt anspricht. Dazu muss man ein sehr lockeres und scharfes „k" formen. Ein nicht zu schweres Blatt erleichtert dies erheblich.

- Am Anfang fühlt sich diese Art von Staccato sehr ungewöhnlich an. Aber nicht aufgeben! Man lernt es schnell!

- Wenn die Übung gelingt, darf das Tempo gesteigert und auch die Dynamik variiert werden.

53. EXERCISES FOR DOUBLE TONGUING

EXECUTION: Play the following exercises in a medium dynamic and at a comfortable tempo:

53. ÜBUNGEN FÜR DIE DOPPELZUNGE

AUSFÜHRUNG: Folgende Übungen in mittlerer Dynamik und einem angenehmen Tempo spielen:

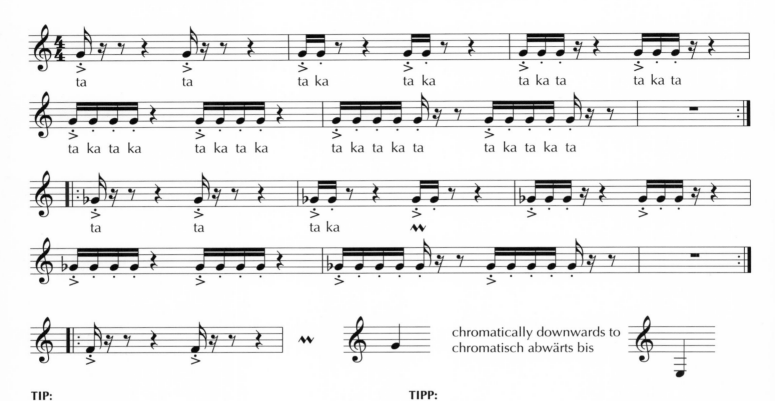

TIP:

✏ Here again the tempo may be increased and the dynamics varied.

TIPP:

✏ Auch hier darf das Tempo gesteigert und die Dynamik variiert werden.

54. EXERCISES FOR DOUBLE TONGUING

EXECUTION: Play the following exercises in a medium dynamic and at a comfortable tempo:

54. ÜBUNGEN FÜR DIE DOPPELZUNGE

AUSFÜHRUNG: Folgende Übungen in mittlerer Dynamik und einem angenehmen Tempo spielen:

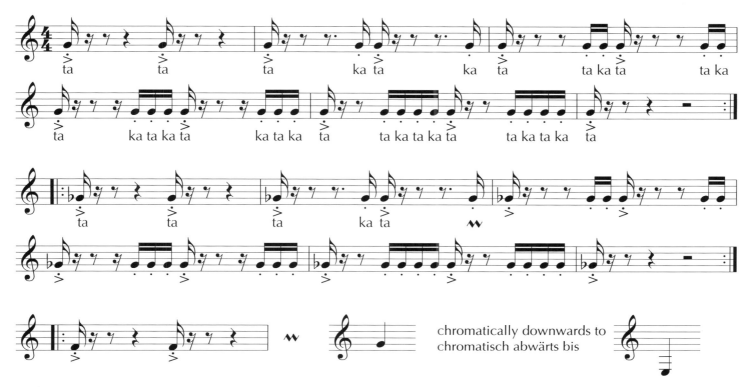

chromatically downwards to
chromatisch abwärts bis

TIPS:

- The exercises are particularly well suited to improving the response on the "ka" (or "ke") syllables. Pay special attention that the response is light, and neither accentuated nor late.

- Here again the tempo may be increased and the dynamics varied.

TIPPS:

- die Übungen eignen sich besonders, um die Ansprache der Silben „ka" (bzw. „ke") zu verbessern. Man achte sehr darauf, dass die Ansprache locker ist, nicht akzentuiert und nicht zu spät.

- auch hier darf das Tempo gesteigert und die Dynamik variiert werden.

55. EXERCISES FOR DOUBLE TONGUING

AIM, EXECUTION and **TIPS** as for exercise no. 52:

55. ÜBUNGEN FÜR DIE DOPPELZUNGE

ZIEL, AUSFÜHRUNG und **TIPPS**
wie bei der Übung Nr. 52.

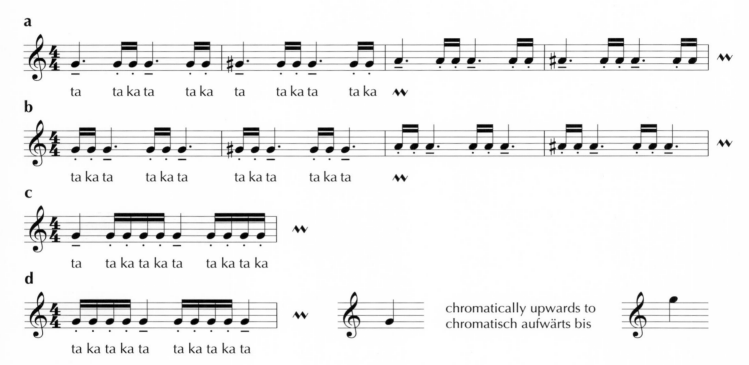

TIP:

✏ Response in the second register is considerably more difficult. No attempt should be made to force the result. Continue practising only to the point where the notes are still speaking well! With a little patience this threshold will shift upwards.

TIPP:

✏ Die Ansprache im zweiten Register ist sehr viel schwieriger. Man sollte nicht versuchen, das Ergebnis zu erzwingen, sondern nur bis dahin üben, wo die Töne noch gut ansprechen! Mit einiger Geduld wird sich diese Grenze nach oben verschieben.

56. EXERCISES FOR DOUBLE TONGUING

AIM, EXECUTION and TIPS as for exercise no. 53:

56. ÜBUNGEN FÜR DIE DOPPELZUNGE

ZIEL, AUSFÜHRUNG und TIPP
wie bei der Übung Nr. 53.

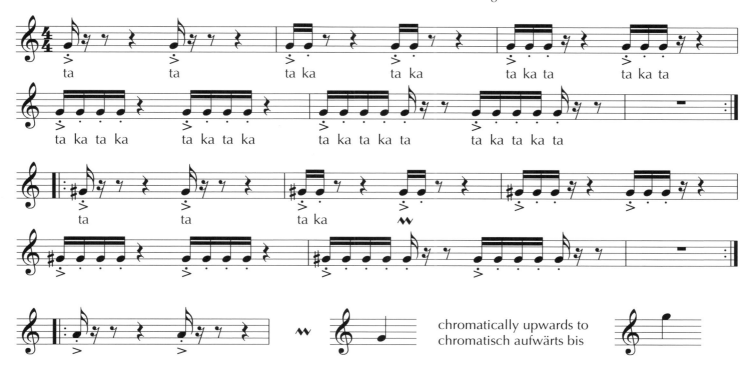

57. EXERCISES FOR DOUBLE TONGUING

AIM, EXECUTION and TIPS as for exercise no. 54:

57. ÜBUNGEN FÜR DIE DOPPELZUNGE

ZIEL, AUSFÜHRUNG und TIPPS
wie bei der Übung Nr. 54.

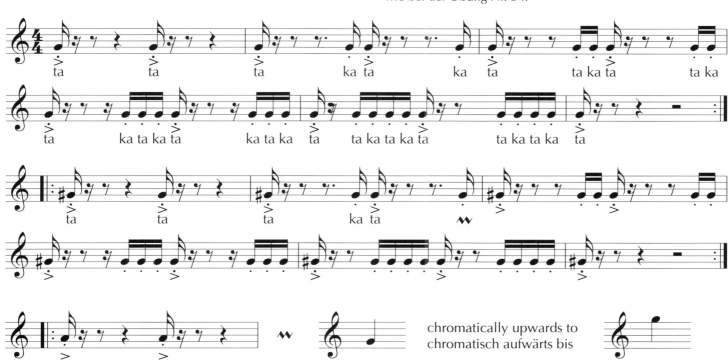

58. EXERCISES FOR DOUBLE TONGUING

AIM: The tongue attack and the fingerwork must fit together with absolute precision. This should be practised taking short note sequences and scale passages that are easy to finger.

EXECUTION: Play the following exercises in a medium dynamic (mp or mf) and at a comfortable tempo (♩ = 112 – 120):

58. ÜBUNGEN FÜR DIE DOPPELZUNGE

ZIEL: Zungenstoß und Greifbewegung müssen absolut präzise zusammenpassen. Dies soll in kurzen Notenfolgen und einfach zu greifenden Skalen geübt werden.

AUSFÜHRUNG: Folgende Übungen in einer entspannten Dynamik (mp oder mf) und in einem angenehmen Tempo (♩ = 112 bis 120) spielen:

TIPS:

✏ For doubletonguing, the coordination of the fingers and the tongue requires a great deal of practice. This needs to be done with care and in a wide range of keys (see exercises no. 24, 26, 28 and 30).

✏ The tempo may be raised steadily.

TIPPS:

✏ Das Zusammenspiel von Fingern und Zunge bedarf bei der Doppelzungentechnik sehr großer Übung. Es sollte sorgfältig in den verschiedensten Skalen geübt werden (siehe Übungen Nr. 24, 26, 28 und 30).

✏ Das Tempo darf kontinuierlich gesteigert werden.

59. EXERCISES FOR DOUBLE TONGUING

AIM: The purpose of this exercise is, once again, the synchronisation of fingers and tongue.

EXECUTION: Play the following exercise in a relaxed dynamic (mp or mf) and at a comfortable tempo (♩ = 112 – 120):

59. ÜBUNG FÜR DIE DOPPELZUNGE

ZIEL: Auch diese Übung dient der Synchronisation von Fingern und Zunge.

AUSFÜHRUNG: Folgende Übung in einer entspannten Dynamik (mp oder mf) und in einem angenehmen Tempo (♩ = 112 bis 120) spielen:

TIPS:

✏ Care must again be taken in the execution of this exercise, which should be extended further using other scale passages (see exercises no. 25, 27, 29 and 31).

✏ Here, too, raise the tempo steadily.

TIPPS:

✏ Auch diese Übung muss sorgfältig ausgeführt und in anderen Skalen weiter weitergeführt werden (siehe Übungen Nr. 25, 27, 29 und 31).

✏ Auch hier das Tempo kontinuierlich steigern.

60. STAMINA EXERCISE FOR DOUBLE TONGUING

AIM, EXECUTION und TIPS as for exercise no. 51.

60. KONDITIONSÜBUNG FÜR DIE DOPPELZUNGE

ZIEL, AUSFÜHRUNG und TIPPS
wie bei der Übung Nr. 51.

Anyone learning the clarinet very soon notices what great – indeed crucial – significance the clarinet reed has for the quality of tone production and articulation. Whilst the experience gained from the first lessons may well be simply that such a reed breaks easily, it is not long before one finds out that some reeds make one struggle endlessly whilst others work distinctly better in all sorts of ways. A good teacher will naturally be able to provide a great deal of help here, which will certainly be necessary. But as progress is made on the instrument, it becomes clear that the problems do not decline but, on the contrary, become more complex. While the player's aspirations concerning tone, intonation and articulation grow – issues that are specifically cultivated and developed in this volume of "Clarinet Fundamentals" – so do the demands made on the clarinet reed! Every player sooner or later naturally develops an idea as to what his or her individual tone should be like. This very individual tone is certainly not wholly dependent on the clarinet reed, but is influenced by the instrument, the mouthpiece (material, facing curvature) and of course crucially also by the player, with his or her own unique qualities. But nonetheless, all clarinettists will have to make two honest admissions: firstly, that when performing they have on many occasions failed to produce their ideal tone, due almost always to the clarinet reed – that most unstable variable in the complex system of tone production; and secondly, that alongside the subjective criteria, there are also objective ones that must be satisfied by all good reeds. However different the demands made on the reed may be (whether it is used to play in a jazz band or in a brass band, 2nd clarinet in a classical orchestra or the solo part in the Nielsen concerto) and however contrasting and individual the desired tone – thankfully – is and should definitely remain (whether the playing is dark in colour or lighter and more brilliant, the tone more powerful and richer in overtones or softer and more malleable), a good reed must in every case have the following qualities:

● **a clarinet reed must sound "clean"** – even in pianissimo and on poor notes, i.e. it must vibrate freely and produce as little extraneous reed noise as possible.

● **it must have tension,** for if the reed tip does not spring back elastically, no clean articulation is possible.

● **the reed must be "open",** which means that irrespective of the facing curvature, it must allow a free and big tone to be produced; the reed underside (bottom table) must not be warped or distorted as this narrows the mouthpiece opening.

● **a reed must not sound hard** and

● **a reed must have warmth and volume** especially in forte, on high notes and with "short fingerings" (throat notes f♯ to b♭).

Now any clarinettist will react to this by saying: "I could do with a reed like that!" but unfortunately it soon becomes clear that such reeds are not always to be had. On the other hand, good reeds are anything but a matter of chance, and it is highly regrettable that as concerns reeds, many clarinettists do not know or observe even the most important of basic rules. But any player who – whether voluntarily or out of ignorance – allows an inferior clarinet reed higher status than his or her

Jeder, der das Spielen der Klarinette erlernt, merkt sehr rasch, welch große – ja entscheidende – Bedeutung das Klarinettenblatt für die Qualität der Tongebung und der Artikulation besitzt. Ist es in den ersten Unterrichtsstunden vielleicht nur die Erfahrung, dass solch ein Blatt sehr zerbrechlich ist, so gewinnt man doch bald schon die Erkenntnis, dass es einerseits Blätter gibt, auf denen man sich unendlich abmüht, und andererseits Blätter, auf denen vieles so deutlich einfacher gelingt. Ein guter Pädagoge wird hier sicherlich wesentliche Hilfestellung geben können und müssen. Im Verlauf des Fortschritts auf dem Instrument zeigt sich aber leider, dass die Probleme nicht kleiner werden, sondern eher komplizierter. Wenn nämlich die Ansprüche an den Klang, die Intonation und die Artikulation größer werden – ein Anliegen, welches gerade durch diesen Band mit „Basisübungen für Klarinette" unterstützt und entwickelt werden soll –, wachsen auch die Ansprüche an das Klarinettenblatt! Selbstverständlich hat jeder Spieler früher oder später auch seine individuelle Vorstellung davon, wie sein Klang sein sollte. Dieser ganz eigene Klang hängt dann sicher auch nicht ausschließlich vom Klarinettenblatt ab, sondern wird beeinflusst vom Instrument, vom Mundstück (Material, Bahnverlauf) und natürlich ganz wesentlich vom Spieler selbst mit seiner Einzigartigkeit. Trotzdem wird jeder Klarinettist erstens ehrlich zugeben müssen, dass er sehr häufig klanglich nicht so gespielt hat, wie er sich das optimal vorstellen würde, was dann fast immer überwiegend am Klarinettenblatt, dieser instabilsten Variablen im komplizierten System der Klangbildung gelegen hat, und zweitens wird auch jeder Klarinettist zustimmen, dass es neben den subjektiven Kriterien auch objektive gibt, die jedes gute Blatt erfüllen muss. Denn auch wenn die Anforderungen an ein Blatt noch so verschieden sein mögen (ob in einer Jazz-Band gespielt wird oder im Blasorchester, ob 2. Klarinette im klassischen Orchester oder der Solopart im Nielsen Konzert) und auch, wenn die Tonvorstellungen (ob dunkel gespielt wird oder heller und glanzvoller, ob der Ton kräftiger und obertonreicher ist oder weicher und biegsamer) Gott-sei-Dank individuell und verschieden sind und unbedingt auch bleiben sollten – ein gutes Blatt muss auf jeden Fall folgende Eigenschaften haben:

● **Ein Klarinettenblatt muss „sauber" klingen** – auch im Pianissimo und auch auf ungünstigen Tönen, d. h. es muss frei schwingen und sollte möglichst wenig Geräuschanteile haben.

● **Es muss Spannung haben,** denn wenn die Blattspitze nicht elastisch federt, ist keine saubere Artikulation möglich.

● **Das Blatt muss „offen" sein,** es muss also einen abhängig vom jeweiligen Bahnverlauf freien und großen Ton ermöglichen und darf daher nicht durch eine verzogene, also verkrümmte Rückseite die Mundstücksöffnung verengen.

● **Ein Blatt darf nicht hart klingen** und

● **ein Blatt muss über Wärme und Volumen verfügen** vor allem im Forte, in der Höhe und auf den „kurzen Griffen" (fis bis b).

Nun wird jeder Klarinettist sagen: „Solch ein Blatt hätte ich auch gern!" Doch wird man leider feststellen müssen, dass es nicht immer gelingt, solch ein Blatt zu haben. Auf der anderen

musical intentions is behaving in a distinctly un-artistic manner. If, on the other hand, the following points are taken to heart, the player's overall reed quality will be raised considerably, and with a little luck a very good reed will always be to hand.

1) THE FORM

A clarinet reed must fit the facing (lay) curvature of the mouthpiece, which varies enormously! Some facings are very short and open (in extreme cases ca. 18 mm long and ca. 1.25 mm open on the Boehm clarinet mouthpiece), some mouthpieces have very long, narrow facings (at maximum ca. 34 mm long and 0.72 mm open in the case of Viennese mouthpieces) and there are, of course, all the different ones between. It is obvious, therefore, that such widely differing facings call for differently formed reeds. The thickness of the blanks, the length of the vamp and the form of the reed "façon" (reed upperside) are important criteria for suiting the reed to the shape of the facing. A mouthpiece with a longer facing calls for a reed with a longer vamp, which in turn (generally speaking) requires a thicker blank. This produces a tone that is rich in overtones but is sometimes also regarded as being a little too bright. In contrast, normally thinner blanks with shorter vamp are played on short, open facings. As a result of the higher vibrating width of the reed and the lower vibrating volume of wood, this open, short facing ideally produces a warm, dark tone which, however, does not sound quite as rich and full in forte. Furthermore, the form of the façon may be 'straighter' (i.e. the sides are not much thinner than the central part of the reed) or 'rounder'. The straighter forms give a clearer tone whilst those that are rounder give a more supple tone but one that is more susceptible to producing extraneous noises. It goes without saying that at first, the clarinet pupil is recommended the appropriate mouthpiece/reed combination by his or her teacher. But should an advanced pupil wish to embark on the search for his or her own individual tone, while trying out a mouthpiece he/she must always question whether the reed 'matches' it. Playing the same standard reed on the most widely differing mouthpieces is senseless. **Mouthpiece and reed make up an inseparable and complementary unit!**

2) THE CANE

The cane for our clarinet reeds comes from a type of giant reed belonging to the family of grasses (Lat.: Arundo Donax), which grows in the temperate climate zones (southern France, Spain, Italy, Turkey, China, Mexiko etc). The cane is harvested in winter and must then be dried carefully over a long period. Good cane is creamy yellow in colour and has even, straight and dense fibres (the so-called xylem = water-transporting vessels). With some experience, it becomes clear to the player that the properties of the cane constitute by far the most crucial factor for the quality of a clarinet reed. Any firm offering clarinet reeds for sale will therefore do its utmost to use the best cane possible. Despite these efforts, the differences between the reeds from one and the same delivery or box and the differences between the individual firms' products are

Seite sind gute Blätter alles andere als ein Zufall, und es ist ausgesprochen bedauerlich, dass viele Klarinettisten in der Frage der Blätter nicht einmal die wichtigsten Grundregeln kennen und beachten. Wer aber – freiwillig oder aus Unkenntnis – seine musikalischen Vorstellungen einem minderwertigen Klarinettenblatt unterordnet, handelt sehr unkünstlerisch. Wenn dagegen die folgenden Punkte beherzigt werden, wird sich sicher das allgemeine Niveau der Blätter erheblich steigern, und mit ein wenig Glück wird auch immer ein sehr gutes Blatt zur Verfügung stehen.

1) DIE FORM

Ein Klarinettenblatt muss zur Mundstücksbahn passen! Mundstücksbahnen sind ausgesprochen verschieden. Es gibt sehr kurze, offene Bahnen (ca. 18 mm lang, ca. 1,25 mm offen im Extrem beim Boehm-Klarinetten-Mundstück), sehr lange, enge Bahnen (ca. 34 mm lang und 0,72 mm offen im Extrem bei Wiener Mundstücken) und natürlich auch alle Zwischenstufen. Es liegt daher nahe, dass so völlig verschiedene Bahnen auch verschieden geformte Blätter erfordern. Die Dicke des Keiles (Blattrohlings), die Länge des Ausstichs und die Form des Blattrückens sind wesentliche Kriterien für eine Anpassung des Blattes an die Form der Bahn. Ein Mundstück mit einer längeren Bahn erfordert ein Blatt mit einem längeren Ausstich, was wiederum (im allgemeinen) einen dickeren Keil voraussetzt. Auf diese Art erzielt man einen obertonreichen Klang, der als kräftig, aber manchmal auch als hell empfunden wird. Im Gegensatz dazu bläst man auf kurzen, offenen Bahnen normalerweise dünnere Keile mit kürzerem Ausstich. Die offene, kurze Bahn erzeugt durch die größere Schwingungsweite des Blattes und das geringere schwingende Holzvolumen dabei im Idealfall einen warmen, dunklen Klang, der aber im Forte nicht ganz so reich und voll klingt. Darüberhinaus kann die Form des Blattrückens eher gerade sein (d. h. die Seiten sind nicht viel dünner als die Blattmitte) oder eher rund. Die geraden Formen geben einen klareren Ton, die eher runden Formen einen weicheren, der aber empfindlich ist für Nebengeräusche. Es ist selbstverständlich, dass der Klarinettenschüler am Anfang die geeignete Kombination Mundstück/Blatt von seinem Lehrer empfohlen bekommt. Sollte sich aber ein fortgeschrittener Schüler auf die Suche nach dem individuellen Klang begeben wollen, so müsste er sich beim Probieren von Mundstücken immer auch fragen, ob er das passende Blatt dazu benutzt. Auf den verschiedensten Bahnen ein immergleiches Standardblatt zu benutzen ist unsinnig. **Mundstück und Blatt sind eine untrennbare, sich ergänzende Einheit!**

2) DAS HOLZ

Das Holz für unsere Klarinettenblätter stammt von einer zur Familie der Gräser gehörenden Riesenschilf-Art (lat.: Arundo Donax), welche in gemäßigten Klimazonen wächst (Süd-Frankreich, Spanien, Italien, Türkei, China, Mexiko usw.). Das Holz wird im Winter geerntet und muss dann sorgfältig über einen längeren Zeitraum getrocknet werden. Gutes Holz hat eine cremegelbe Farbe, gleichmäßige, gerade verlaufende und dichte Fasern (die sogenannten Xyleme = wasserführende

great, and not every reed can satisfy truly high requirements. Various factors are responsible for this. For one thing, as a result of today's high demand, the classic areas of cultivation in the Mediterranean region can no longer meet the world-wide needs and additional cane has to be purchased from a host of different countries and regions of the world; for another, the climate change is already having a clearly negative impact on the quality of the cane as the (too) warm winters are causing the reed plants to start growing too early. Added to this is the fact that cultivation (with planting density, fertilizing and irrigation), harvest, drying, storage and further processing represent considerable cost factors and – in a similar manner as with viniculture – quality and quantity are, apparently irreconcilably, mutually exclusive. In this situation, the best advice for the up-and-coming clarinettist is to build up knowledge and critical awareness. A professional wind-player is strongly advised to acquire a measuring device for determining the hardness of the cane. By using only reeds of moderate cane hardness, as is advantageous, one can save oneself a great deal of time, strain and money.

3) BREAKING IN

Nowadays there are few clarinet reed producers left who still moisten, check and scrape to adjust the underside of their reeds over a period of days before delivering them to their clients. This is the ideal case since reeds from these firms are considerably more regular in terms of strength and stability of the underside. But today, most manufacturers supply reeds which have never been exposed to moisture. **The constant alternation between the wet and dry state places an extraordinarily great strain on a small piece of wood!** It is thus of the utmost importance to use caution when acclimatizing new reeds to moisture. During the first few days, in particular, careful attention should be paid to ensuring that the contrast between wet state and dry state should not be too stark. A new reed should neither be saturated completely nor allowed to dry out completely afterwards. Hence, a new reed must neither be played for a long period nor left in water for minutes at a time. It is advisable not to play the reeds at all on day one, two or three, but merely to dip them **briefly** into water, dry them and leave them alone. A will of steel is of course needed to resist trying out new reeds as soon as they are delivered, but the more care and restraint one exercises in preparing the reeds to take the strain of being played, the better they will repay this with quality and length of useful life. After these initial days, the underside should be checked by placing the moistened reed on a polished sheet of glass and wet-grinding it, if needed, using a precise and fine grindstone (experience shows that this is necessary in the case of almost all reeds that have not received this treatment beforehand from the maker); the reeds should then be sorted according to their strength and tone quality. From this point onwards the reeds are played each day and the playing time may be increased little by little from ca. 5 minutes at first; in addition, the order of the reeds is constantly rearranged according to quality. Here, a learning process should definitely be taking place concerning the point from which a reed no longer

Gefäße) und eine mittlere Holzhärte. Man wird mit einiger Erfahrung feststellen, dass die Beschaffenheit des Holzes mit Abstand der entscheidende Faktor für die Qualität eines Klarinettenblattes ist. Jede Firma, die Klarinettenblätter anbietet, wird daher auch bestrebt sein, möglichst gutes Holz zu verwenden. Trotzdem sind die Unterschiede zwischen den Blättern ein- und derselben Lieferung oder Packung und auch die zwischen den Angeboten der einzelnen Firmen sehr groß, und nicht jedes Blatt kann wirklich hohen Ansprüchen genügen. Dafür sind verschiedene Faktoren verantwortlich. Zum einen führt die Quantität des weltweiten Verbrauchs heute dazu, dass die klassischen Anbaugebiete in den Mittelmeerländern nicht mehr ausreichen und Holz aus den verschiedensten Ländern und Erdteilen dazugekauft werden muss, zum anderen beeinflusst bereits deutlich der Klimawandel mit zu warmen Wintern, in denen die Rohre zu früh wachsen, negativ die Qualität des Holzes. Hinzu kommt, dass Anbau (mit Anbaudichte, Düngung und Bewässerung), Ernte, Trocknung, Lagerung und Weiterverarbeitung große Kostenfaktoren darstellen, und – ähnlich wie beim Weinanbau – sich Klasse und Masse offenbar unversöhnlich gegenseitig ausschließen. Dem angehenden Klarinettisten kann in dieser Situation nur geraten werden, sich Kenntnisse und Kritikfähigkeit anzueignen. Einem professionellen Bläser ist darüber hinaus dringend zu empfehlen, sich ein Messgerät zur Bestimmung der Holzhärte zuzulegen. Wenn man nur Blätter mit der günstigen, mittleren Holzhärte verwendet, spart man sehr viel Zeit, Nerven und Geld.

3) DAS EINSPIELEN

Es gibt nur noch wenige Hersteller von Klarinettenblättern, welche die Blätter, bevor sie an die Kunden ausgeliefert werden, über mehrere Tage befeuchten, kontrollieren und die Unterseite nachschleifen. Dies stellt den Idealfall dar, denn die Blätter dieser Firmen sind wesentlich konstanter in der Stärke und in Bezug auf die Stabilität der Unterseite. Bei den meisten Blätterherstellern allerdings bekommt man heutzutage Blätter, welche noch nie der Feuchtigkeit ausgesetzt waren. **Der ständige Wechsel zwischen Nässe und Trockenheit ist aber eine unglaubliche Belastung für ein kleines Stück Holz!** Es ist daher von allergrößter Wichtigkeit, neue Blätter behutsam an die Feuchtigkeit zu gewöhnen. Gerade in den ersten Tagen sollte unbedingt darauf geachtet werden, dass der Unterschied zwischen Feuchtigkeit und Trockenheit nicht zu groß wird. Ein neues Blatt sollte also weder völlig durchfeuchtet werden, noch danach wieder vollständig austrocknen. Daher darf man ein neues Blatt weder längere Zeit spielen noch minutenlang ins Wasser legen. Es empfiehlt sich, an den ersten zwei oder drei Tagen die Blätter gar nicht zu spielen, sondern nur **kurz** ins Wasser zu tauchen, dann wieder abzutrocknen und ruhen zu lassen. Es erfordert natürlich eiserne Selbstdisziplin, neu gelieferte Blätter nicht gleich auszuprobieren, aber je behutsamer und sorgfältiger man die Blätter auf ihre Belastungen vorbereitet, desto mehr danken sie es mit Qualität und Lebensdauer. Nach diesen ersten Tagen kontrolliert man die Unterseite des Blattes, indem man es angefeuchtet auf eine plangeschliffene Glasscheibe legt, schleift sie gegebenen-

improves. After three or four days the breaking-in phase is over and one should part with reeds that, despite now being even on the underside and having received any necessary adjustments (see no. 10), still do not produce a satisfactory tone: a heroic step indeed!

4) THE REED STRENGTH

The optimal reed strength depends on the player's individual wishes and the types of playing involved. Reed strength is normally defined in numbers (Strength 2, 2 ½, 3, 3 ½, 4), whereby the effective strength obviously depends on the opening of the mouthpiece. A reed of Strength 4 used on a narrow facing is not, therefore, necessarily very hard. But whatever facing and reed strength one elects to play, one point should not be forgotten: **As a result of breaking in the reeds, the tension in the cane is further diminished and the strength is normally reduced considerably.** Since, in addition to this, it is necessary to further grind down the underside of practically all new reeds, new reeds must be somewhat too hard at first. The true strength of a reed can only be assessed after three or four days, therefore, and is a matter of much experience. Many clarinettists are delighted when the reed functions well on the first day, only to find afterwards that their reeds are almost always softer than they would wish. It should be noted, in addition, that reeds react very strongly to air pressure and humidity. Reeds become much harder at high altitudes and with high humidity, whilst in dry weather and at low altitudes they are softer. Thus it often happens that in winter, with low humidity in heated rooms, one's reeds are far too soft.

5) REGULARITY

Clarinet reeds are living material. They wear out quickly if played too much but equally react unfavourably if not played for days or weeks on end. Many a player, wishing to keep a superb reed alive, has preserved it "to death". It is thus advisable to play the reeds regularly at least for a few minutes. In this way, the reeds never dry out completely, the changes they undergo are kept to a minimum, and the player keeps track of the quality of his or her reeds. Selecting a reed will always be a game of chance for any player who is not completely familiar with his reeds and their changing states!

6) STORAGE

The storage of the reeds in current use is of crucial importance. Since one needs to know every reed individually, a simple cardboard box is totally unsuitable. A reed case with a clear dividing system is a must. Most reed cases have glass sheets as underlays for the reeds. Here, however, it is not advisable to lay the reeds on the glass plate while they are still very wet, as they stick to the glass while drying. In this case air is prevented from coming into contact with the underside of the reed, considerably raising the danger of it warping. It is preferable to lay the reed on its reverse side so as to allow it to dry for a few minutes before putting it into the case, so that it does not adhere to the glass. Some reed cases have grooved plastic as the underlay, which is more suitable for achieving even drying of the reeds. It should in all cases be possible to

falls auf einem präzisen Schleifstein nass nach, was erfahrungsgemäß bei nahezu allen Blättern, die nicht auf diese Weise schon beim Hersteller vorbehandelt wurden, nötig ist, und sortiert die Blätter dann nach der Stärke und der Tonqualität. Von nun an bläst man die Blätter jeden Tag, wobei man die Spieldauer von anfangs ca. 5 Minuten nach und nach steigern darf und ordnet immer wieder auch die Reihenfolge der Blätter nach Qualität. Dabei sollte unbedingt durch Erfahrung gelernt werden, wann ein Blatt nicht mehr besser werden wird. Denn nach drei oder vier Tagen ist die Einspielphase vorbei, und von Blättern, die dann trotz gerader Unterseite und eventuell nötigen Nachbehandlungen (siehe bei Nr. 10) nicht befriedigend klingen, sollte man sich heldenhaft trennen.

4) DIE BLATTSTÄRKE

Die optimale Blattstärke richtet sich nach den individuellen Vorstellungen und Aufgabenbereichen des Bläsers. Die Blattstärken werden meistens mit Ziffern bezeichnet (Stärke 2, 2½, 3, 3½, 4), wobei die effektive Stärke logischerweise abhängig ist von der Öffnung des Mundstücks. Ein Blatt mit der Stärke 4 muss also auf einer engen Bahn nicht unbedingt sehr schwer sein. Aber egal, welche Bahn und Blattstärke man blasen möchte, eines darf nie vergessen werden: **Durch das Einspielen der Blätter löst sich im Holz noch Spannung, und die Stärke lässt in der Regel deutlich nach.** Da man zudem die Unterseite fast aller neuen Blätter noch nachschleifen muss, müssen neue Blätter etwas zu schwer sein. Die wirkliche Stärke eines Blattes lässt sich also erst nach etwa drei bis vier Tagen beurteilen, und die Einschätzung der Stärke eines neuen Blattes ist eine Sache von viel Erfahrung. Viele Klarinettisten freuen sich, wenn das Blatt am ersten Tag richtig geht und haben danach fast immer Blätter, welche leichter sind, als sie es sich wünschen. Darüber hinaus sollte noch bemerkt werden, dass Blätter auch sehr deutlich auf den Luftdruck und die Luftfeuchtigkeit reagieren. In großen Höhenlagen und bei hoher Luftfeuchtigkeit werden Blätter viel schwerer, bei trockenem Wetter und in geringen Höhenlagen dagegen leichter. So kommt es auch, dass man im Winter bei der geringen Luftfeuchtigkeit in geheizten Räumen häufig viel zu leichte Blätter hat.

5) DIE REGELMÄSSIGKEIT

Klarinettenblätter sind lebendes Material. Sie verschleißen schnell, wenn man zu viel auf ihnen spielt, sie vertragen es aber meist auch nicht, tage- oder sogar wochenlang nicht gespielt zu werden. Sicherlich ist so manches wunderbare Blatt von seinem Spieler schon „zu-Tode-geschont" worden. Es ist also günstiger, die Blätter regelmäßig wenigstens für einige Minuten zu spielen. Die Blätter trocknen dann nie vollkommen aus, die Veränderungen am Blatt werden dadurch minimiert und der Bläser behält die Übersicht über die Qualität seiner Blätter. Wer nicht alle seine Blätter mit den ihnen eigenen Veränderungen genau kennt, für den wird die Blattsuche immer ein Glücksspiel sein!

close the reed case effectively, so that the reeds are stored in their own micro-climate and not affected negatively by the air in the room, which is usually far dryer. Nowadays, reed cases fitted with a humidifier and hygrometer are available. Storing the reeds at around 70 % relative air humidity results in a considerably higher reed quality and significantly longer life. Reed cases may also be stored in a 'Humidor' (originally intended for the storage of cigars).

7) THE UNDERSIDE

It has already been pointed out more than once that the underside of a reed must stay flat. Herein lies the crux of the problems, alas, since unlike the double reed of the oboe and bassoon, where the two halves of the reed stabilize one another, the entire tip of the clarinet reed vibrates in the air freely. If one considers that even thick planks warp if subjected to moisture, the existence of clarinet reeds that maintain their flat underside at all is something of a miracle. But unfortunately, it can also happen that an excellent reed – one that has been handled regularly and wisely – warps repeatedly, thereby becoming unusable. All clarinettists thus require a polished glass plate for checking and a very fine grindstone for corrections. Warping can occur in three fundamental ways:
a) The reed warps longways. Sticking the moistened but not overmoist reed onto the glass plate shows that only the tip and the end of the reed lie flat. A reed thus distorted very significantly narrows the opening of the mouthpiece. After scraping, this distortion occurs very frequently on the following day, too, which means that it is then irreparable: After scraping for a second time, at the latest, it is time to part with such a reed!
b) The reed warps at the sides. With the reed on the glass plate, observed lengthwise the reed lies flat in the middle with the sides curled upwards. This type of warping results in a highly impure tone. After correction on the grindstone, the reed does not normally warp again in this manner, so this is the easiest defect to put right.
c) The reed warps in waves longways. This distortion is most unpleasant as it occurs only after the reed has been played for a few minutes. After playing, the reed gradually becomes increasingly hard. On the glass plate, the tip and a middle portion of the reed lies flat. This type of distortion is caused by tensions in the cane and thus in many cases often recurs. This third type of distortion is, however, not all that common.

8) THE NUMBER

Clarinettists have been known to go on tour taking only two reeds with them. However much one may admire this 'fatalism', seen from the perspective of common sense this approach is, at best, daredevil. But the opposite case of a clarinettist trying to find a usable reed from 50, ten minutes before the concert begins, is not particularly intelligent either. We can therefore conclude that the solution must lie somewhere in the middle. The "ideal" number of reeds cannot, of course, be precisely stated, but one should in any case sort one's reeds into three categories. On one side (perhaps, quite literally, of the reed case) are the reeds that are broken in and

6) DIE AUFBEWAHRUNG

Von größter Wichtigkeit ist die Aufbewahrung der in Gebrauch befindlichen Blätter. Da man jedes einzelne Blatt kennen muss, ist eine einfache Pappschachtel völlig ungeeignet. Ein Etui mit einer erkennbaren Einteilung ist eine Notwendigkeit. Die meisten Etuis enthalten Glasplatten als Unterlage für die Blätter. Es ist dann aber nicht günstig, die Blätter völlig nass auf die Glasplatte zu legen, so dass das Blatt beim Trocknen am Glas anklebt. In diesem Fall bekommt das Blatt von unten keine Luft mehr, und die Gefahr des Verziehens der Unterseite steigt erheblich. Besser ist es, das Blatt vor dem Einlegen in das Etui wenige Minuten auf dem Blattrücken liegend antrocknen zu lassen, damit es nicht am Glas festklebt. Andere Blätteretuis haben Plastikrillen als Unterlage, was für das gleichmäßige Trocknen der Blätter günstiger ist. Auf jeden Fall sollte das Etui gut verschließbar sein, damit die Blätter in einem eigenen Mikroklima lagern und nicht von der meist viel trockeneren Raumluft negativ beeinflusst werden. Es gibt inzwischen auch schon Blätteretuis, die mit Befeuchtern und Hygrometer ausgestattet sind. Eine Lagerung der Blätter bei etwa 70 % relativer Luftfeuchtigkeit führt zu deutlich höherer Qualität der Blätter und auch zu einer wesentlich längeren Haltbarkeit. Man kann auch seine Blätteretuis in einem Humidor (ursprünglich für die Lagerung von Zigarren vorgesehen) aufbewahren.

7) DIE UNTERSEITE

Dass die Unterseite eines Blattes immer gerade sein muss, wurde schon mehrfach angesprochen. Hier liegen leider auch die größten Probleme, denn anders als beim Doppelrohr von Oboe oder Fagott, wo sich die beiden Rohrhälften gegenseitig stabilisieren, schwingt die gesamte Spitze des Blattes frei in der Luft. Wenn man bedenkt, dass sich selbst dicke Bretter nach Feuchtigkeitseinwirkung krümmen, ist es eigentlich ein Wunder, dass es Klarinettenblätter gibt, die ihre gerade Unterseite behalten. Aber es kann eben auch leider passieren, dass ein wunderbares Blatt, welches man mit Regelmäßigkeit und Klugheit behandelt hat, sich immer wieder verzieht und dadurch unbrauchbar wird. Jeder Klarinettist muss daher also über eine geschliffene Glasscheibe zur Kontrolle und einen sehr feinen Schleifstein zum Korrigieren verfügen. Es gibt drei Grundarten des Verziehens:
a) Das Blatt verzieht sich der Länge nach. Wenn man das angefeuchtete, aber nicht zu nasse Blatt auf die Glasplatte klebt, wird auf der Rückseite deutlich, dass nur die Spitze und das Blattende anliegen. Ein in dieser Weise verzogenes Blatt verengt ganz deutlich die Öffnung des Mundstücks. Sehr häufig tritt dieses Verziehen nach dem Schleifen auch am nächsten Tag wieder auf. Es ist dann irreparabel und man sollte sich spätestens nach dem zweiten Schleifen von solch einem Blatt trennen!
b) Das Blatt verzieht sich seitlich. Auf die Glasplatte gelegt, sieht man der Länge nach die Mitte anliegen und die Seiten hochgewölbt. Diese Art des Verziehens macht den Ton sehr unsauber. Meist verzieht sich ein Blatt nach der Korrektur auf dem Schleifstein nicht wieder in dieser Weise. Daher ist dieser Fehler am ehesten zu beheben.

have been successfully "tried and tested" in rehearsals, concerts or lessons. They have been played for at least a week and their strengths and weaknesses are known to the player. No further significant change is to be expected: the reeds are reliable.

An amateur should have two or three such reeds and a professional perhaps twice that number. These are moistened regularly but otherwise one spares them the wear-and-tear of use while practising. In addition to these "real thing" reeds, one's reed case should contain just as many reeds with their initial breaking-in days behind them, and practise on these daily. If they prove to be good in practice, they are tried out in rehearsals and, in positive cases, transferred to the side of the "real thing" reeds. A third (and last) category consists of new reeds one is breaking in with care. This category should consist of 10 reeds at most, as the player should be dealing with them on a daily basis (cf. no. 3 "Breaking in"). To sum up, the important elements are firstly, precise knowledge of each individual reed and its development; secondly, sorting one's reeds wisely and on the basis of experience within the categories; and thirdly, sensing the moment when a reed should, come what may, be thrown out. All in all, an amateur would have a total of 6 to 10 reeds and a professional around 20. A much higher number than this makes no sense **as good reeds do not result from sheer quantity, but rather through skilful "reed management".**

9) THE TIMING

One of the gravest errors made in the whole reed context is surely the easiest to put right: A great many clarinettists fail to order new reeds in good time! As long as one still has a certain number of good reeds available, the need to arrange for new reeds does not seem a real necessity. **But the search for reeds is also a considerable psychological strain!** And never does one find better reeds than when one still has some good ones anyway, and never does the search seem more hopeless than when none of one's reeds work and a reed is needed urgently! So let us allow wisdom to prevail! Reeds need systematic and thus also regular preparation. And just a little shrewdness leads the player to order new reeds while he or she still has one – or for that matter several – new boxes at home: Suppliers' unavoidable delivery delays are especially long when they are at their most unwelcome!

10) ADJUSTMENT

All that has been said so far leads us to conclude that "ready-for-use" or "off-the-peg" reeds do not exist. The wind-player must always be in a position to react to changes in the material. As already noted, a glass sheet and a grindstone are needed for correction of the reed underside. Provided that one can buy a carefully produced reed model that fits one's own mouthpiece, not a great deal of processing should be necessary on the upperside of the reed, in other words on the façon. After a certain period the pores of the cane may become highly prominent, which can be corrected using very fine sandpaper. But, due especially to the necessary grinding of the underside, the reed very commonly becomes a great deal sof-

c) Das Blatt „verwirft" sich der Länge nach. Dieses Verziehen ist sehr unangenehm, weil es erst eintritt, nachdem man das Blatt einige Minuten gespielt hat. Das Blatt wird beim Spielen nach und nach immer schwerer. Auf der Glasplatte sieht man die Spitze und einen mittleren Teil des Blattes anliegen. Auch diese Art des Verziehens liegt an Spannungen im Holz und tritt daher häufig immer wieder auf. Allerdings ist diese dritte Art des Verziehens nicht sehr häufig.

8) DIE ANZAHL

Es hat schon Klarinettisten gegeben, die mit nur zwei Blättern auf Tournee gingen. So sehr man diesen Fatalismus bewundern mag, vernünftig betrachtet ist dieses Verhalten allenfalls tollkühn. Das Gegenteil allerdings, dass ein Klarinettist zehn Minuten vor dem Konzert versucht, aus 50 Blättern ein brauchbares herauszufinden, ist ebenfalls nicht sonderlich intelligent. Wir schließen daraus, dass die Lösung in der Mitte liegen muss. Die „ideale" Anzahl von Blättern lässt sich natürlich nicht genau angeben, aber man sollte auf jeden Fall seine Blätter in drei Kategorien einteilen. Auf der einen Seite (vielleicht sogar wörtlich zu nehmen: auf der einen Seite des Blätteretuis) die eingespielten Blätter, die sich schon, sei es bei Proben, Konzerten oder im Unterricht, bewährt haben. Sie sind mindestens schon eine Woche gespielt, dem Bläser in ihren Stärken und Schwächen vertraut und verändern sich auch nicht mehr wesentlich. Sie sind verlässlich.

Von diesen Blättern sollte ein Amateur zwei oder drei besitzen, ein Profi vielleicht doppelt so viele. Man wird sie regelmäßig befeuchten aber ansonsten nicht beim Üben verschleißen. Neben diesen „Ernstfallblättern" sollte man noch einmal so viele Blätter im Etui haben, die ihre ersten Einspieltage hinter sich haben und auf denen man täglich übt. Wenn sie sich dabei bewähren, werden sie bei Proben getestet und wechseln im positiven Fall auf die Seite zu den „Ernstfallblättern". Eine dritte (und letzte) Kategorie betrifft die neuen Blätter, die man behutsam einspielt. Diese Kategorie sollte höchstens 10 Blätter beinhalten, weil man sich ja täglich mit ihnen beschäftigen sollte (vgl. Nr. 3 „Das Einspielen"). Zusammenfassend kann man feststellen: Wichtig sind erstens die genaue Kenntnis jeden einzelnen Blattes mit seinen Entwicklungen, zweitens ein kluges und erfahrenes Sortieren innerhalb der Kategorien und drittens ein Gefühl für den Zeitpunkt, an dem man ein Blatt definitiv wegwerfen sollte. Zusammengenommen käme ein Amateur auf eine Blätterzahl von 6 – 10 Blättern und ein Profi auf etwa 20. Vielmehr ist nicht sinnvoll, denn **nicht die reine Quantität schafft gute Blätter, sondern ein geschicktes „Blätter-Management".**

9) DAS TIMING

Einer der gravierendsten Fehler in der Blätterfrage ist sicher am leichtesten abzustellen: Sehr viele Klarinettisten versäumen es, rechtzeitig neue Blätter zu bestellen! Man verspürt eben nicht so recht die Notwendigkeit, sich um neue Blätter zu kümmern, während noch einige gute Blätter vorhanden sind. **Aber die Blättersuche ist auch eine große psychische Belastung!** Und nie findet man bessere Blätter, als wenn man schon einige gute hat, und nie scheint alles aussichtsloser, als

ter than one would wish. Where the reed becomes only slighter softer, this can be put right by attaching it to the mouthpiece somewhat higher up. But if the alteration in strength is too great, a reed cutter is needed, a tool available in specialist shops. Any façon should be able to accommodate a small part (less than 0.5mm) being cut off. If, on the other hand, a larger portion has to be cut off, some adjustment of the façon will be needed, as the removal has changed the curvature and the tone produced by the reed is generally harder. For fine-adjusting the façon (and also, of course, for fine-adjusting reeds that are too hard in the first place) a fine file (nowadays special files made of glass are available for clarinet reeds), a reed knife (available in specialist shops) or dried field horsetail (Equisitum arvense) is used. It is almost impossible to go into the fine adjustment from a theoretical perspective and it requires a vast amount of experience. Here, nevertheless, are some important hints:

a) Fine-adjustment is most successful if carried out with very strong side illumination. Sunlight coming from the side is ideal, but, alternatively, a good lamp will also suffice. In this light, it is possible to see the surface of the reed very clearly. A quality reed looks very good from the side, i. e. no jagged places, edges, bumps or grooves are visible, but rather the regular curve of the façon. Incidentally, from the side it is also possible to see whether the façon is flatter or rounder in form.

b) It is scarcely ever the case that both sides of a reed are equally hard. One tests the sides by turning the mouthpiece slightly to the right or left when blowing. This allows one side to vibrate freely, whilst the other is being hindered from vibrating. Obviously, in the case of reeds that are too hard, the thickness of the harder side must be reduced first.

c) The reed tip must always be flexible and rich in tension. One must beware of filing off too much from the tip of the reed. Both sides of the reed tip can be tested for flexibility if one bends them upwards while the reed is in a wet state. If the sides cannot be bent upwards readily, the reed is far too hard. But if they do not spring back immediately and with elasticity, the tip is too thin and the reed has no tension.

d) The fine-adjustment of reeds is purely a matter of experience. A reed consists of living material. Even if it were possible to make reeds with thousandth-millimetre precision, they would still vary greatly. It is important that one has the confidence to gather one's own experience. The opportunity to do some experimentation is offered with reeds that, following the playing-in period, one already intends to reject. Having once experienced the pleasure of rendering playable an apparently hopeless reed, one may perhaps discover that working with reeds is bound up with playing the clarinet in an inseparable and positive way.

wenn keins mehr geht und man dringend eines bräuchte! Daher lasse man Klugheit walten! Blätter macht man mit System, also regelmäßig. Und mit ein wenig Intelligenz bestellt man auch schon neue Blätter, wenn man noch eine oder mehrere neue Packungen zuhause hat, denn die unvermeidlichen Lieferzeiten der Händler sind gerade dann besonders lang, wenn man es überhaupt nicht gebrauchen kann!

10) DAS NACHARBEITEN

Aus allem bisher Gesagten entnehmen wir, dass es keine „fertigen Blätter" gibt. Der Bläser muss immer in der Lage sein, auf die Veränderungen des Materials zu reagieren. Es wurde schon angesprochen, dass man zur Korrektur der Unterseite eine Glasscheibe und einen Schleifstein benötigt. Vorrausgesetzt, dass man für seine spezielle Mundstücksbahn ein passendes und mit Sorgfalt hergestelltes Blättermodell kaufen kann, sollte an der Oberseite des Blattes, also an der Facon, nicht viel zu bearbeiten sein. Es könnten nach einiger Zeit die Poren des Holzes sehr stark hervortreten, was man mit sehr feinem Schleifpapier korrigieren kann. Ein sehr häufiger Fall ist aber, gerade auch bedingt durch das notwendige Glattschleifen der Unterseite, dass das Blatt deutlich leichter wird, als man es sich wünscht. Ein geringfügiges Leichter-Werden kann man noch beheben, indem man das Blatt auf dem Mundstück etwas weiter oben befestigt. Ändert sich die Stärke jedoch zu viel, so braucht man einen im Fachhandel erhältlichen Blattabschneider. Ein geringes Abschneiden (unter 0,5mm) sollte jede Facon problemlos vertragen. Wenn man dagegen mehr abschneiden muss, muss man die Facon etwas nacharbeiten, da sich durch das Abschneiden der Kurvenverlauf geändert hat und das Blatt meistens dadurch härter klingt. Zum Nacharbeiten der Facon (natürlich auch zum Nacharbeiten von Blättern, die schon von alleine zu schwer sind) benutzt man eine feine Feile (inzwischen gibt es spezielle Feilen aus Glas für Klarinettenblätter), ein im Fachhandel erhältliches Rohrmesser oder getrockneten Schachtelhalm. Das Nacharbeiten entzieht sich nahezu gänzlich einer theoretischen Erörterung und bedarf sehr großer Erfahrung. Trotzdem an dieser Stelle einige wichtige Hinweise:

a) Das Nacharbeiten gelingt am besten in einem sehr starken Seitenlicht. Ideal ist seitliches Sonnenlicht, eine gute Lampe tut es aber auch. In diesem Licht kann man von der Seite sehr gut die Oberfläche des Blattes betrachten. Ein gutes Blatt sieht von der Seite sehr gut aus, d. h. es sollten keine Ecken, Kanten, Beulen oder Rillen zu erkennen sein, sondern ein gleichmäßiger Verlauf der Kurve der Facon. Man kann von der Seite übrigens auch gut erkennen, ob die Facon mehr gerade ist oder eher rund.

b) Es sind fast nie beide Seiten eines Blattes gleich schwer. Man testet die Seiten, indem man beim Blasen das Mundstück ein wenig im Mund nach rechts oder links verkantet. Dadurch lässt man jeweils eine Seite frei schwingen, während man die andere verstärkt abdämpft. Logischerweise muss man bei zu schweren Blättern zuerst die schwerere Seite leichter machen.

c) Die Blattspitze muss immer flexibel sein und voller Spannkraft. Man muss sich hüten, an der Spitze des Blattes viel weg-

zufeilen. Man kann beide Seiten der Blattspitze auf die Flexibilität testen, wenn man sie einzeln im feuchten Zustand nach oben biegt. Lassen sie sich schon schwer nach oben biegen, ist das Blatt viel zu schwer. Federn sie aber nicht gleich wieder elastisch zurück, ist die Spitze zu dünn und das Blatt hat keine Spannung.

d) Das Nacharbeiten von Blättern ist eine reine Erfahrungssache. Ein Blatt besteht aus lebendem Material. Auch, wenn es gelänge, das Blatt auf den Tausendstel Millimeter genau herzu-

stellen, würde es immer noch große Unterschiede geben. Wichtig ist, dass man sich traut, eigene Erfahrungen zu sammeln. Es bietet sich doch geradezu an, an den Blättern, die man nach den Einspieltagen schon aufgeben möchte, ein wenig herumzuarbeiten! Wenn man dann einmal erfahren hat, wie schön es ist, einem eigentlich hoffnungslosem Blatt zu gut spielbaren Zustand verholfen zu haben, wird man vielleicht auch erkennen, dass die Arbeit mit den Blättern untrennbar und auch positiv mit dem Klarinettenspiel verbunden ist!

Recommended Reading · Literaturempfehlungen | 7

MUSIC:

Fridthjof Christoffersen (ed.): Tägliche Studien aus Carl Baermanns „Clarinett-Schule" op. 63
Studies with scales, arpeggios and intervals in all keys.
The book of clarinet "vocabulary"!
Verlag Hoffmeister, Leipzig, Nr. 8015

Fritz Kroepsch: 416 Etüden für Klarinette in fortschreitender Ordnung, Part 1 and Part 2
The standard work of exercises written in the classical and romantic harmonic system
C. F. Schmid Verlag, Renningen

Alfred Uhl: 48 Etüden für Klarinette (2 Volumes)
Highly musical and expressive studies proving that however sophisticated the technical issues might be, technique must always take second place to the music itself. A **must** for all up-and-coming clarinettists.
Schott, Mainz, KLB 12 / 13

Paul Jean-Jean: Études Progressives et Mélodiques (3 Volumes)
One slow and one fast study in each key. The slow studies are good performance pieces and are useful for training stamina and shaping interpretation; the fast are good practice for avoiding stiffness.
Verlag Alphonse Leduc, Paris

Johann Sebastian Bach / Ulysse Délecluse: Quinze Études
Difficult and exhausting but the most wonderful music to practise!
Verlag Alphonse Leduc, Paris

Rudolf Jettl: Der vollkommene Klarinettist, (3 Volumes)
Very difficult and swarming with accidentals including double flats and sharps, extended harmonic range, each study in a particular musical vein. The summit of the learning process.
Verlag Josef Weinberger, Wien

NOTEN:

Fridthjof Christoffersen (Hrsg.): Tägliche Studien aus Carl Baermanns „Clarinett-Schule" op. 63, Tonleitern, Rückungen, Akkorde und Intervallstudien in allen Tonarten.
Das „Vokabelbuch" für Klarinette!
Verlag Hofmeister, Leipzig, Nr. 8015

Fritz Kroepsch: 416 Etüden für Klarinette in fortschreitender Ordnung, Teil 1 und Teil 2
Das Standardwerk mit Übungen im klassisch-romantischen Modulationssystem.
C. F. Schmid Verlag, Renningen

Alfred Uhl: 48 Etüden für Klarinette (2 Bände)
Ausgesprochen musikalische und ausdrucksstarke Etüden, die bei allen differenzierten technischen Schwierigkeiten beweisen, dass sich die Technik der Musik unterzuordnen hat. Ein **Muss** für jeden angehenden Klarinettisten.
Schott, Mainz, KLB 12 / 13

Paul Jean-Jean: Études Progressives et Mélodiques (3 Bände)
Jeweils eine langsame und eine schnelle Etüde pro Tonart. Die langsamen Etüden sind schöne Vortragsstücke, gut für Kondition und Gestaltung; die schnellen sind gut für die Lockerheit.
Verlag Alphonse Leduc, Paris

Johann Sebastian Bach / Ulysse Délecluse: Quinze Études
Schwierig und anstrengend, aber die wunderbarste Musik zum Üben!
Verlag Alphonse Leduc, Paris

Rudolf Jettl: Der vollkommene Klarinettist, (3 Bände)
Sehr schwierig, sehr viele Vorzeichen, auch Doppelvorzeichen, erweiterte Harmonik, jede Etüde in ganz eigenem musikalischem Charakter. Der Endpunkt einer Ausbildung.
Verlag Josef Weinberger, Wien

Beate Zelinsky / David Smyers (ed.): Pro Musica Nova, Studien zum Spielen Neuer Musik (German/English)
Detailed introduction to playing techniques employed in new music based on numerous examples from the works of major composers (e.g. Denissow, Scelsi, Lachenmann, Xenakis). Well-researched bibliography, recommended compositions, discography.
Verlag Breitkopf und Härtel, Wiesbaden, Nr. EB 8589

BOOKS IN ENGLISH:

Oskar Kroll: The Clarinet
Informative and to the point; every clarinettist should own a copy; many illustrations, bibliography.
B. T. Batsford Ltd., London, 1968
Taplinger, New York, 1968

Jack Brymer: The Clarinet (Yehudi Menuhin Music Guides)
Detailed account of the history, acoustics, practice of playing, literature and clarinet tuition, detailed references to the literature.
Kahn&Averill, London, 2005
ISBN 1-871082-12-9
Schirmer, New York, 1976

Colin Lawson (Editor): The Cambridge Companion to the Clarinet
12 separate chapters on various themes relating to the clarinet by renowned clarinettists. Sound and highly informative. Numerous illustrations, valuable references.
Cambridge University Press, 1995
ISBN 47668 2 paperback
ISBN 47066 8 hardback

Albert R. Rice: The Baroque Clarinet
The most extensive and significant publication on this subject. Interesting and extensive literature recommendations.
Clarendon Press, Oxford, 1992
ISBN 0 19 816188 3

Paul Newhill: The Basset-Horn and its Music
The book by the best authority on the basset horn.
Rosewood Publications, Bradfield, 2003

Colin Lawson: Mozart Clarinet Concerto
Anyone who intends to play this work should have read this book. Latest update on the complex history of the origin of this, the most exquisite of clarinet concertos. Numerous illustrations.
Cambridge University Press, 1996
ISBN 0-521-47929-0

Beate Zelinsky / David Smyers (Hrsg.): Pro Musica Nova, Studien zum Spielen Neuer Musik (dt./engl.)
Ausführliche Einführung in die Spieltechniken Neuer Musik anhand von vielen Beispielen bedeutender Kompositionen (u. a. Denissow, Scelsi, Lachenmann, Xenakis).
Fundiertes Literaturverzeichnis, Kompositionsempfehlungen, Diskografie.
Verlag Breitkopf und Härtel, Wiesbaden, Nr. EB 8589

BÜCHER IN DEUTSCHER SPRACHE:

Conny Restle / Heike Fricke (Hrsg.): Faszination Klarinette
Ein wunderbares Buch über 300 Jahre Klarinette. Viele Photos, interessante Artikel, **das** Buch für jeden Klarinetten-Fan.
Prestel Verlag, München (2004)
ISBN 3-7913-3180-9

Oskar Kroll: Die Klarinette
Informativ und sachlich, sollte jeder Klarinettist besitzen, viele Abbildungen, Literaturverzeichnis.
Bärenreiter Verlag, Kassel
ISBN 3-7618-0086-X

Jack Brymer: Die Klarinette (in der Reihe: „Yehudi Menuhins Musikführer") Ausführliche Darstellung von Geschichte, Akustik, Praxis, Literatur und Klarinettenunterricht, ausführliche Literaturhinweise.
Fischer Taschenbuch Verlag
ISBN 3-596-22986-3

Dr. Josef Saam: Das Bassetthorn, seine Erfindung und Weiterentwicklung.
Das Standardwerk über das Bassetthorn.
Schott, Mainz

Thomas Grass / Dietrich Demus: Das Bassetthorn
Ausführlich recherchiert und beschrieben.
Riesige Literaturliste. Das Buch für den Bassetthorn-Liebhaber
Eigenverlag
ISBN 3-8311-4411-7

Bruno Bartolozzi: Neue Klänge für Holzblasinstrumente
Immer noch ein Standardwerk mit vielen Griffbeispielen für Vierteltöne und Mehrklänge.Die Griffangaben leider nur für Boehm-System.
Schott Verlag, Mainz

Gerhard Krasnitzer: Multiphonics für Klarinette mit deutschem System und andere zeitgenössische Spieltechniken.
In seiner Ausführlichkeit und Systematik nicht zu schlagen. Allerdings nur für das Oehler-System. Beiliegende CD mit Beispielen.
Edition Ebenos
ISBN 3-9808379-0-4

BOOKS IN ENGLISH:

Bruno Bartolozzi: New Sounds for Woodwinds
Remains a standard text with many fingering examples for quarter tones and multiple tones
Oxford University Press, 2005
ISBN 0 19318611 X

Richard Gilbert: The Clarinettists' Discography III
A wealth of biographies, many photos and thousands of recordings.
RGProductions, New Jersey, 1991

Pamela Weston: Clarinet Virtuosi of the Past
Stadler, Hermstedt, Baermann, Crusell, Mühlfeld and others – Magnificently researched, grippingly written.
Fentone Music Limited, Corby, 1971 / 1994

Pamela Weston: More Clarinet Virtuosi of the Past
Fenton Music Limited, Corby, 1977 / 1982
ISBN 0 9506259 1 4

Pamela Weston: Clarinet Virtuosi of Today
An important reference work, almost 50 biographies, many photos.
Egon Publishers Ltd., Baldock, 1989
ISBN 0 905858 46 8

Michele Gingras: Clarinet Secrets
A host of valuable tips and ideas on playing technique.
Scarecrow Press
ISBN 0-8108-4791-2

Eloise Ristad: A Soprano on her Head
On making music and stage fright.
Real People Press
ISBN 0-911226-21-4

Peter Hadcock: The Working Clarinetist
Orchestral studies with comments
Roncorp Publications
ISBN 0-939103-05-2

Roberto Braccini: Praktisches Wörterbuch der Musik
Gives four languages – Italian, English, French and German – on the same page. An essential item for all musicians. Well organised with a good index.
Schott, Mainz
ISBN 3-7957-827

BÜCHER IN DEUTSCHER SPRACHE:

Eugen Brixel : Klarinetten Bibliographie I
Fast 500 Seiten Literaturverzeichnis von Solo bis zum großen Kammerensemble. Standardwerk.
Verlag Heinrichshofen, Wilhelmshaven
ISBN 3-7959-0144-8

Werner Richter: Bewußte Flötentechnik – Versuch einer ganzheitlichen Darstellung
Ausgesprochen kenntnisreiches Buch über eine bläserische Ausbildung. Die Kapitel über Physik, Akustik, Nerven/Organe, Verhalten/Bewegung/Haltung, Atmung/Atemtechnik / Atemstütze und Artikulation sind in ihrer genauen Darstellung von höchster Wichtigkeit für jeden Bläser.
Musikverlag Zimmermann, Frankfurt
ISBN 3-921729-31-9

Margot Scheufele-Osenberg: Die Atemschule
Ausführliche Anleitung zum Erlernen richtiger Atmungs-, Haltungs- und Stützarbeit. Sehr wichtig für jeden Bläser.
Schott, Mainz 1998
ISBN 3-7957-8705-X

Renate Klöppel: Die Kunst des Musizierens
Sehr tiefgehende Behandlung der physiologischen und psychologischen Grundlagen des Übens und der Funktion von Nervensystem und Sinnesorganen.
Schott, Mainz 1993 / 1997
ISBN 3-7957-8706-8

Gerhard Mantel: Einfach Üben
Viele gute Ideen und Rezepte. Die Kapitel über Bewegungen mehr für Cellisten, aber alles andere ist sehr wertvoll für jeden Musiker.
Schott, Mainz 2001 / 2004
ISBN 3-7957-8724-6

Gerhard Mantel: Mut zum Lampenfieber
Sehr nützliches Buch mit umfassender Analyse der Probleme und guten Strategien zu ihrer Bewältigung! Sollte man nicht erst lesen, wenn es fast zu spät ist!
Schott, Mainz 2003 / 2005
ISBN 3-254-0835-7

Doris Geller: Praktische Intonationslehre für Instrumentalisten und Sänger
Unglaublich gutes Buch, bei dem einem „die Ohren aufgehen". Sehr detaillierte Erklärungen, viele ganz ausgezeichnete Übungen, zugehörige CD. Dieses Buch sollte jeder Musiker gelesen haben!
Bärenreiter Verlag, Kassel
ISBN 3-7618-1265-5
CD : ISBN 3-7618-1266-3

BOOKS IN ENGLISH:

Robert Jourdain: Music, the Brain and Ecstasy
A music book with a difference. It is only when the brain becomes involved that sounds are converted into music! Jourdain traces the path from the sound, via the note, melody, harmony, rhythm and composition, all the way to (possible) ecstasy. Entertaining yet also highly informative.
Harper Collins Publishers Inc., New York, 1997
ISBN 0-380-78209-X

BÜCHER IN DEUTSCHER SPRACHE:

Roberto Braccini: Praktisches Wörterbuch der Musik
In Italienisch, Englisch, Französisch und Deutsch viersprachig auf der gleichen Seite. Unverzichtbar für jeden Musiker. Gute Systematik, gutes Register.
Schott, Mainz
ISBN 978-3-254-08279-4

Frederic Vester: Denken, Lernen, Vergessen
Was geht in unserem Kopf vor, wie lernt das Gehirn, und wann lässt es uns im Stich?
dtv Verlag, München
ISBN 3-421-02672-6

Robert Jourdain: Das wohltemperierte Gehirn
Ein etwas anderes Musikbuch. Erst das Gehirn macht aus Klängen Musik!
Joudain schildert den Weg vom Schall über den Ton, die Melodie, die Harmonie, den Rhythmus, die Komposition bis zum Verstehen und zur (möglichen) Ekstase. Unterhaltsam, aber sehr informativ.
Spektrum Akademischer Verlag, Heidelberg, Berlin
ISBN 3-8274-0224-7